A Michigan Polar Bear
Confronts the Bolsheviks

Private Godfrey Anderson. The patch on his left shoulder
indicates that he posed for this portrait after returning to
Detroit with his fellow "Polar Bears." (Godfrey Anderson
Collection, Grand Rapids Public Library)

A Michigan Polar Bear
Confronts the Bolsheviks

A War Memoir

The 337th Field Hospital
in Northern Russia, 1918-1919

Godfrey J. Anderson

Edited and with
an Introduction by

Gordon L. Olson

WILLIAM B. EERDMANS PUBLISHING COMPANY
GRAND RAPIDS, MICHIGAN / CAMBRIDGE, U.K.

Published 2010 by
Wm. B. Eerdmans Publishing Co.
2140 Oak Industrial Drive N.E., Grand Rapids, Michigan 49505 /
P.O. Box 163, Cambridge CB3 9PU U.K.

Printed in the United States of America

15 14 13 12 11 10   7 6 5 4 3 2 1

Library of Congress Cataloging-in-Publication Data

Anderson, Godfrey J., 1895-1981.
    A Michigan polar bear confronts the Bolsheviks: a war memoir:
  the 337th Field Hospital in northern Russia, 1918-1919 / Godfrey J. Anderson;
  edited and with an introduction by Gordon L. Olson.
        p.   cm.
      Includes bibliographical references and index.
      ISBN 978-0-8028-6520-5 (pbk.: alk. paper)
      1. Anderson, Godfrey J., 1895-1981. 2. United States. Army.
  American Expeditionary Forces. Field Hospital, 337th. 3. Polar Bear Expedition
  (1918-1919) 4. Soviet Union — History — Allied intervention, 1918-1920.
      5. Soviet Union — History — Revolution, 1917-1921 — Personal narratives, American.
      6. Soviet Union — History — Revolution, 1917-1921 — Participation, American.
      7. Soviet Union — History — Allied intervention, 1918-1920 — Medical care.
  I. Olson, Gordon L.   II. Title.
  DK265.42.U5A528   2010
  947.084′1 — dc22

                                            2010031092

www.eerdmans.com

Contents

Acknowledgments

This is Godfrey Anderson's memoir, and it is important to me to recognize the care with which he organized and wrote about his experiences in northern Russia. Godfrey's wife, Ruth, and son, Robert, supported his interest, and had he been able to bring his memoir to print during his lifetime, he would have first thanked them for supporting his decision to undertake the writing. I am honored to do so here.

As I researched Godfrey Anderson's story, I received assistance from many librarians and archivists. At the Grand Rapids Public Library, Rebecca Main, Chris Byron, Jennifer Morrison, Marcella Beck, and Timothy Gleisner facilitated my access to Anderson's papers and photographs, and helped locate other background information and photographs.

Anderson deposited a portion of his memoir in the Bentley Historical Library at the University of Michigan, where archivists placed it in the Polar Bear Expedition Digital Collections. Conceived by Professor Elizabeth Yakel of the University of Michigan's School of Information, the collection brings together more than sixty "Polar Bear" document collections and published materials. Anyone can access the collection's Web site (http://polarbears.si.umich.edu/). Also helpful for research is the "Detroit's Own" Polar Bear Memorial Association Web site (http://pbma.grobbel.org/), maintained by Mike Grobbel, which provides links to many other Polar Bear-related Web sites.

The best collection of photographs relating to the Allied North Russia Expedition is in the U.S. Army Signal Corps collection at the splendid National Archives facility in Suitland, Maryland. Holly Reed, of the Archive's still photos section, responded quickly and helped me make very profitable use of a day scanning photos that provide a visual complement to Anderson's narrative.

My friend Frank N. Schubert read and commented on the entire manuscript, and readers are the beneficiaries of his thoughtful insights.

Godfrey Anderson's memoir went relatively unnoticed for many years, until Bill Eerdmans, president of Eerdmans Publishing Company, agreed that it deserved publication. Once he decided to publish Godfrey's memoir, his company's skilled staff took over. Editor Reinder Van Til, who had advocated for this book's publication, edited my introductions to the memoir. Designer Klaas Wolterstorff turned the manuscript and a pile of photographs into a book — a process that amazes me as much now as it did when I began my career as a historian over forty years ago. Willem Mineur brought the same skill and creativity to the cover design.

Finally, and most important, I want to thank my wife, Christine, for her patience and encouragement. As a graduate student, I developed a persistent habit of working late into the night. It has been my remarkable good fortune that long ago Christine accepted that and my many other idiosyncrasies.

GORDON L. OLSON
Grand Rapids, Michigan,
July 2010

Preface

I MET GODFREY ANDERSON in 1978, shortly after I had become the city historian of Grand Rapids, Michigan. The city had celebrated the 150th anniversary of its founding that year, two years after the 1976 national celebration of the Bicentennial of the Declaration of Independence. As those celebratory years drew to a close, city commissioners decided they would try to sustain the heightened popular interest in history by establishing the city historian position. My job consisted of collecting historical information and materials, creating publications about the history of the Grand River Valley, and initiating educational programs. Upon taking that position, I was interviewed for a *Grand Rapids Press* story and told a reporter that veterans of twentieth-century military service were one of the human sources from whom I hoped to gather documentary material and oral histories. Shortly after that story ran, Godfrey Anderson called to tell me he had written a memoir of his World War I experience in northern Russia, and if I would be interested, I could stop by and pick it up. I was delighted to receive that call and quickly made an appointment for what turned out to be the first of several visits, with Godfrey ultimately presenting his memoir, his historical photographs, and other archival materials to the Grand Rapids Public Library's local history collections.

When we first met, Godfrey and I discovered that, in addition to the history of Grand Rapids, we shared interests in our common

Swedish heritage, the American Civil War, and baseball. He had played baseball as a young man, including a spring game among the troops in Russia, and had during his life assembled a large library of Civil War and Abraham Lincoln books. We talked for much of the afternoon, and when it came time to part, we agreed to meet again for a more formal, recorded interview session.

Our second session featured a wide-ranging recorded conversation that included talk of his Swedish immigrant parents, who, though they both lived near Sparta, Michigan, had improbably met at the World's Columbian Exhibition in Chicago. We also talked about his youth in West Michigan, his World War I experience, and his life in Grand Rapids after the war. Outside of his family, Godfrey spoke most enthusiastically about his library and the pleasure he derived from reading and studying history. He made it clear that, while he valued the camaraderie of military life and had enjoyed the brief weeks his unit spent in England, there were no such fond memories of the cold winter and the time he spent as a member of the 337th Field Hospital Unit fighting during the winter of 1918-1919 in northern Russia. He spoke with deep respect for the American, British, and Canadian soldiers who had performed valiantly, but he did not believe the mission had been well conceived or had had much chance of success.

It was not until late in his life that Godfrey Anderson chose to write a memoir of his World War I experience, and when he did, he relied primarily on his memory to describe his induction and basic training. It is clear that, for his time in England and Russia, he turned to some published accounts to complement his memory. In some cases he describes English locations that he passed in his troop train in the dark of night, which he clearly would have liked to have seen were he a tourist rather than a soldier. Because these early segments of the memoir tend to read like a travelogue and are not an integral part of Anderson's narrative as a soldier, I have chosen to separate them from the main text and place them, instead, in Appendices A and B at the end of this book.

In some instances Anderson also turned to other published accounts for background information when he wrote of his experience in the American Expeditionary Force North Russia (regularly referred to as the Allied North Russian Expedition, and popularly known as the

"Polar Bear Expedition"). Like any ordinary soldier, what he saw and heard limited his personal understanding of what transpired. To give a broader perspective to the events of that winter, he turned to books such as *The American Expedition Fighting the Bolsheviki: Campaigning in North Russia, 1918-1919,* written by Captain Joel R. Moore, Lieutenant Harry H. Mead, and Lieutenant Lewis E. Jahns (published in Detroit in 1920). However, I want to emphasize that most of this memoir came exclusively from Godfrey's memories, and what he wrote adds valuable insights into his work in the 337th Hospital Unit.

With very few exceptions, Eerdmans is publishing this memoir as Godfrey Anderson physically wrote it. He was a careful writer with a straightforward, transparent style, and in publishing his work verbatim, I have retained his capitalization, punctuation, and grammatical idiosyncrasies in order to preserve authorial authenticity. I have added occasional explanatory footnotes below the text, and have used brackets in the text itself to note my corrections or questions. Because part of the manuscript was still in Godfrey's original handwriting, there were a few instances where a word was unclear; in these cases, brackets identify my best understanding of the word he intended.

By writing his memoir, Godfrey Anderson provided an invaluable resource for those seeking to understand the soldier's life in the North Russia Expedition. He wrote not to glorify his participation in the expedition, but so that future generations would remember the men he served with and cared for. When he turned over his manuscript to the Grand Rapids Public Library, I promised Godfrey Anderson that I would do what I could to get it published. Now, nearly three decades later, with the help of William B. Eerdmans and the staff at Eerdmans Publishing Company, I am honored to be able to fulfill that promise.

IN 1982, Dennis Gordon included an excerpt from this memoir in his book *Quartered in Hell: The Story of the American North Russian Expeditionary Force, 1918-1919.* Also in 1982, I edited and used a short segment of the memoir for the *Grand River Valley Review,* published by the Grand Rapids Historical Society. Interestingly, Anderson divided his memoir into two sections. The portion describing his Russian experience is in the Bentley Historical Library at the University of Michigan; he deposited his description of basic training and traveling to Europe in the Grand Rapids History and Special Collections Department of the Grand Rapids Public Library. Now the two sections of his carefully crafted work are available in this single volume to readers and researchers.

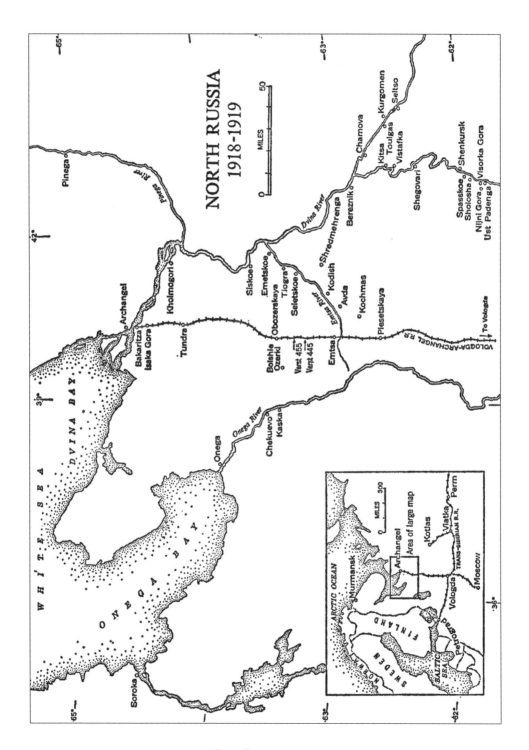

NORTH RUSSIA
1918-1919

MILES
0   50

White Sea
Dvina Bay
Onega Bay

Pinega
Pinega River
Archangel
Bakaritza
Isaka Gora
Kholmogori
Tundra
Siskoe
Emetskoe
Obozerskaya
Tiogra
Seletskoe
Bolshie Ozerki
Verst 455
Verst 445
Emtsa
Emtsa River
Avda
Kodish
Kochmas
Plesetskaya
Shredmehrenga
Bereznik
Dvina River
Chamova
Kitsa
Toulgas
Vistafka
Kurgomen
Seltso
Shegovari
Spasskoe
Sholosha
Nijni Gora
Ust Padenga
Shenkursk
Visorke Gora
To Vologda
VOLOGDA-ARCHANGEL R.R.
Onega
Onega River
Chekuevo
Kaskac
Soroka

ARCTIC OCEAN
Murmansk
NORWAY
SWEDEN
FINLAND
BALTIC SEA
Petrograd
Vologda
Moscow
Kotlas
Viatka
Perm
TRANS-SIBERIAN R.R.
Archangel
Area of large map
MILES
0   300

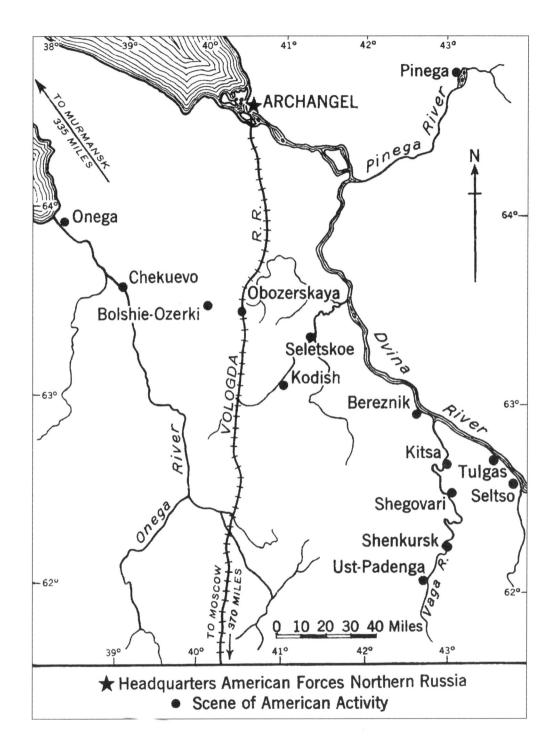

★ Headquarters American Forces Northern Russia
● Scene of American Activity

Woodrow Wilson and the Use of American Troops

WHEN THEY BEGIN, government policy and military strategy decisions are about theories, philosophies, and ideas; as they make their way toward implementation, however, they become about individuals — the men and women assigned to carry them out. President Woodrow Wilson and Private Godfrey Anderson represent the two opposing poles of that chain of command as it played out in northern Russia in 1918-1919. On May 29, 1918, Anderson, a young West Michigan farm boy, bade his parents good-bye and reported to the military induction office in Holland, Michigan, to begin serving in the United States Army. When the nation had entered World War I a year earlier, Anderson had dutifully registered for the draft. After completing his initial processing, he moved on to basic training at Camp Custer in Battle Creek, Michigan.

Throughout his basic training and initial stationing days as a member of a hospital unit in England, Anderson had a military experience like that of most other American soldiers in World War I. Unbeknownst to him, however, President Wilson was about to make a decision that would send him and five thousand other American soldiers on a dangerous mission to northern Russia. Little known at the time — and seldom remembered after the war — this mission was generally known to the public as the "Polar Bear Expedition," though its official designation was the Allied North Russia Expedition.

On July 17, 1918, six weeks after Anderson had begun his career as a soldier, and while he was still in basic training, President Wilson drafted a confidential memorandum directing American troops to occupy the Russian cities of Archangel, in the far northwest of the country, and Vladivostok, far to the south and east in Asian Russia. Two months later, in early September 1918, Anderson, by then assigned to the 337th Hospital Unit, was on his way to Archangel.

Wilson's memorandum, entitled "Aide Memoire," declared his rationale for sending approximately five thousand U.S. troops to Archangel and eight thousand to Vladivostok.[1] Long-standing treaty commitments tied Russia to Great Britain and France at the beginning of the twentieth century in an alliance generally known as the Triple Entente. Aligned against the entente, Germany, Austria-Hungary, and the Ottoman Empire formed an opposing diplomatic triumvirate known as the Triple Alliance. With nearly every other European nation allied with one side or the other, it took only the push of Gavrilo Princip, a revolutionary Bosnian Serb, and his assassination of Archduke Franz Ferdinand of Austria and his wife, Sophie, the duchess of Hohenberg, on June 28, 1914, in Sarajevo, to trigger a diplomatic domino reaction. When Austria-Hungary responded to the assassination by declaring war on Serbia and her ally, Russia, Germany followed suit on Austria-Hungary's side, causing Great Britain and France to join the war in honor of their treaty obligation to Russia. Thereafter, nation after nation fell in line, until thirty-three nations — including such distant entities as Siam and Costa Rica — joined the fray.[2]

For the next three years, the two groups of treaty-bound nations battled each other, while the United States, separated from the belligerents by the Atlantic Ocean, stayed out of the war. Despite President Wilson's promise to keep his nation out of combat, pressure

1. Wilson's "Aide Memoire," dated July 17, 1918, is reprinted in many places, including General William S. Graves, *America's Siberian Adventure* (New York: Jonathan Cape and Harrison Smith, 1931), pp. 5-10. Because of its top-secret classification, Secretary of War Newton Baker carried the document by train halfway across the country to Kansas City, where he personally handed it to General William S. Graves, assigned to command U.S. troops in eastern Russia.

2. Sage History: An American Experience, Web site created at Northern Virginia Community College in 1995: http://www.sagehistory.net/worldwari/docs/declarationswwi.htm.

to join the war on the side of the Triple Entente heightened in the United States, until a combination of Germany's unrestricted submarine warfare and its misguided effort to recruit Mexico into the Triple Alliance finally convinced Wilson to declare war, which he did on April 6, 1917.

From the beginning of the conflict, Russia's presence on the side of the Western powers forced Germany and her allies to fight a war on two fronts, a thousand miles apart: a western front in France and an eastern line that ran from eastern Poland on the north to Romania, Serbia, and Montenegro on the south. Although Russia's troops were poorly led and ill equipped, the topography they occupied made them a difficult foe. Even after they suffered severe losses in 1915 and 1916 — and many units mutinied — the sheer number of Russian troops demanded the attention of a significant number of Triple Alliance troops.

Germany and her allies wanted Russia out of the war, but they were unsuccessful until Czar Nicholas abdicated his throne in the face of widespread domestic unrest. Wartime shortages and military defeats had exacerbated long-standing economic and social problems under the czar, and that emboldened dissenters to call for his removal. Unable to right his listing ship of state, Nicholas abdicated in March 1917, ending three hundred years of the Romanov dynasty.

An interim government led by leftist Alexander Kerensky attempted to continue Russia's participation in the Triple Entente. But mounting military losses, domestic opposition, and the fear of a German advance on Moscow undermined the new government's authority. Hoping to capitalize on this situation, Germany secretly transported Vladimir Lenin, the Bolshevik leader since 1903, out of exile in Switzerland back to St. Petersburg, where he led a successful takeover of the government by the Social Democratic Workers' Party (popularly known as the Bolsheviks), which plunged Russia from unrest and dissention deep into a civil war. Knowing that he needed to devote all his resources to solidify his hold on power — and indebted to the Germans for their assistance — Lenin negotiated the one-sided Treaty of Brest-Litovsk in March 1918: it gave up a great deal of territory and took Russia out of the war. Lenin simultaneously repudiated Western loans made to previous Russian governments and nationalized foreign investments, further alienating governments of the Western Allies.[3]

Woodrow Wilson had hoped that the Kerensky government would solidify the notion of a democratically elected representative government in Russia. Intellectually, he supported the struggle against the czar, and he supported the Russian people's right to self-determination. He had declared, in his famous January 1918 "Fourteen Points Speech," that among the United States' conditions for peace in Europe was "the evacuation of all Russian territory" by foreign troops, and for Russia to have "an unhampered and unembarrassed opportunity for the independent determination of her own political development and national policy." But since he was ideologically opposed to Bolshevism, Wilson detested the circumstances of Lenin's takeover, and he also worried about support for the Russian Revolution among radicals and Eastern European immigrants in the United States. Furthermore, he and fellow Triple Entente leaders David Lloyd George of Great Britain and Georges Clemenceau of France worried that, if Lenin and the Bolsheviks succeeded and withdrew Russia from the war, it would enable Germany to turn all her power against the members of the Triple Entente nations. They hoped that, by providing aid and assistance to the anti-Bolshevik side in the civil war, they could keep weapons and military supplies out of the hands of the Red Army.[4]

Events were moving swiftly in the spring and early summer of 1918, focusing partly on the former royal Romanov family, whose members were playing the role of pawns in a murderous chess game. They were initially held near St. Petersburg, but they were later transported east

3. There are numerous sources recounting the Russian Revolution and the Bolshevik takeover. Maureen Perrie, ed., *Cambridge History of Russia,* vol. 3 (New York. Cambridge University Press, 2006), offers a good survey in the form of essays by well-regarded scholars; Sheila Fitzpatrick, *The Russian Revolution* (New York: Oxford University Press, 1982) is an excellent concise history, as is W. Bruce Lincoln, *Passage through Armageddon: The Russians in War and Revolution, 1914-1918* (New York: Simon and Schuster, 1986). Essays based on newly opened Soviet archives and close cooperation between Western and Russian scholars can be found in Edward Acton, Vladimir Cherniaev, and William G. Rosenberg, eds., *A Critical Companion to the Russian Revolution, 1914-1921* (Bloomington: Indiana University Press, 1997).

4. David Fogelsong, *America's Secret War against Bolshevism* (Chapel Hill, NC: University of North Carolina Press, 1995), p. 11

beyond the Ural Mountains to the town of Yekaterinburg, where they were held in the house of a local merchant. Concerned about czarist loyalists who were seeking to use the czar as a rallying point, Russia's new government debated his future. Their hand was forced when a large contingent of Czech fighters that was affiliated with Great Britain and the Triple Entente Allies made their way west all the way from Vladivostok to a point near Yekaterinburg, where they threatened to free the czar if they were to come further.

The Czechs had been in Russia since the beginning of World War I. They initially fought as part of Czar Nicholas's army because they had been offered independence from the Austro-Hungarian Empire in return for their service. They formed an independent Czech legion within the Russian army, and their numbers had grown to thirty or forty thousand by 1918. When the Bolsheviks seized power, however, these Czechs saw their dream of independence for their nation evaporate as the eastern front collapsed and the Bolshevik government concluded a separate peace with the Germans and the Triple Alliance. Determined to fight on, the Czech Legion first headed east toward Vladivostok, where ships would take them to France and the western front. As they got close to their goal, however, they encountered Bolshevik fighters, and they turned back to join anti-Bolshevik forces in western Russia.

With the Czechs approaching from the east, Lenin's government in St. Petersburg decided to eliminate the czar and his family from the complicated Russian equation. In the early morning hours of July 17, 1918, Bolshevik guards took the royal family and four of their servants to a basement room, where they shot them and stabbed them to death with their bayonets. Elements of the Czech Legion reached Yekaterinburg days after the execution of the czar and his family, too late to change the course of events.[5]

5. Pavel Medvedev was one of the Bolshevik soldiers assigned to guard the royal family. His account of the execution first appeared in George Gustav Telberg and Robert A. Wilton, *The Last Days of the Romanovs* (New York: George H. Doran Co., 1920). For the next eighty years, rumors persisted that at least one child survived the execution and there were always some who gave those rumors credence. Finally, in the late 1990s, searchers found the bodies, and subsequent DNA testing established their identity beyond all doubt. Accounts of the discovery and testing can be found in Robert K. Massie, *The Fate of the Romanovs: The Final Chapter* (New York: Random

That is where matters stood in the midsummer of 1918. As they watched matters unfold in Russia, members of Wilson's administration were split over U.S. intervention in that country. Initially opposed, Secretary of State Robert Lansing came to support sending American troops to Russia, while Secretary of War Newton Baker and other military leaders preferred to see the troops sent to France. In the end, Wilson sided with Lansing and ordered 5,000 soldiers to Archangel to join about 7,000 British, Canadian, and Australian troops, and about 2,000 French fighters. He assigned an additional 8,000 Americans to Vladivostok, where they joined a like number of Japanese to oppose Bolshevik troops and Cossack marauders who regularly attacked the Trans-Siberian Railroad. It was a tenuous collaboration: the Americans were watching to make sure that the Japanese government did not take advantage of the unstable political environment to gain access to the resource-rich Siberian regions along the railroad.[6]

Woodrow Wilson's hesitance to use troops in Russia was not because he had not deployed troops before. By the time he decided to intervene in Russia, he had demonstrated a willingness to use United States troops as part of his foreign policy on more than one occasion. In 1914, he sent the navy to Vera Cruz, Mexico, in opposition to General Victoriano Huerta, who had seized power from Venustiano Carranza. The following year, when a popular uprising deposed Haitian dictator Jean Vilbrun Guillaume Sam and threatened to replace him with Dr. Rosalvo Bobo, who would undermine Haitian government ties to American business interests, Wilson sent 300 U.S. marines to Port-au-Prince to "protect American and foreign" interests. In 1916 he sent marines to the other side of Hispaniola to establish order in the Dominican Republic. It was also in 1916, in what is probably his best-known intervention, Wilson sent General John J. Pershing to Mexico on a punitive mission after rebel Francisco "Pancho" Villa's forces crossed the New Mexican border and killed sixteen residents of Columbus, New Mexico.[7]

House, 1995), pp. 6-8, 134-35; see also "The Execution of Tsar Nicholas II, 1918": www.eyewitnesstohistory.com (2005).

6. Robert L. Willett, *Russian Sideshow* (Washington, DC: Brassey's, 2003), pp. 166-67, 170; Gibson Bell Smith, "Guarding the Railroad, Taming the Cossacks: The U.S. Army in Russia, 1918-1920," *Prologue* 34, no. 4 (Winter 2002): 294-305.

7. Fogelsong, *America's Secret War*, p. 11.

Sending troops was the last and most assertive of several steps that President Wilson took as he sought to stabilize the Russian government and keep its troops in the war. He maintained an active spy network inside the country while he publicly supported, first the czar, and then the Kerensky government. Soon after war broke out, he joined other Western nations in sending large quantities of aid to the Russians. In 1917 alone, the United States transported nearly $1 billion in guns and equipment to eastern Russia to protect the vital east-west Trans-Siberian Railroad; further, it established the Russian Railway Service to send engineers and technicians, three hundred locomotives, and more than 10,000 railroad cars to boost the system's capabilities.[8]

By 1918, with those vast stores of materiel and large quantities of aid in jeopardy, Wilson felt compelled to participate in forming the Allied North Russia Expeditionary Force. The "Aide Memoire," which he drafted to explain his decision, suggests that Wilson had serious reservations about the action and its prospect for success. He acknowledged that the intervention "would add to the present sad confusion in Russia . . . [and] be of no advantage in the prosecution of our main design, to win the war against Germany." But he concluded that intervention was permissible to "steady efforts at self-government or self-defense in which the Russians themselves may be willing to accept assistance [and] . . . to guard military stores which may subsequently be needed by Russian forces in the organization of their own self-defense."[9]

IN THE MEANTIME, Godfrey Anderson, assigned to the 337th Hospital Unit, had arrived in England, where he expected to spend the remainder of the war caring for the wounded who were being transported from France. He was soon to learn that he would be part of the group

8. Smith, "Guarding the Railroad," pp. 294-305.

9. When Secretary of War Newton Baker delivered his copy of the "Aide Memoire" to General Graves in Kansas City, and informed the latter that he would be leading the U.S. troops destined for Siberia, he said that the "Aide Memoire" "contains the policy of the United States in Russia which you are to follow. Watch your step; you will be walking on eggs loaded with dynamite." Graves, *America's Siberian Adventure,* pp. 1-10.

selected to carry out Wilson's intervention policy. Great Britain had led the effort to station troops in Archangel, and the United States and France were following her lead. The Treaty of Brest-Litovsk between Germany and the revolutionary Leninist leadership separated the Baltic states — Belarus, Ukraine, and Finland — from Russia and granted them independence. And when Germany moved to establish trading relationships with those countries, Great Britain's leaders became concerned that the move would jeopardize their long-standing trading access to the region's vast natural resources and agricultural products. When Germany sent troops into the region, Great Britain's leaders responded by sending British marines to Murmansk, on the Kola Peninsula near the Finnish border. However, the British did not believe that they could secure the region alone, and they pressured their allies to send additional troops. Because the United States troops were fresh and well supplied, they became Great Britain's primary candidates for Russian service. But British leaders did not want to relinquish control of the expedition. Thus did they manage to convince Wilson that — for one of the very few times in its history — the United States would send troops to serve outside the country under the command of generals from another country.

The British plan also depended on the Czech forces making their way west on the Trans-Siberian Railroad. They were to proceed as far as Vologda, about 300 miles due south of Archangel, and then turn north to join British, American, and French troops to form a 50,000-man occupation force. Although the Czechs never made it to Vologda, their promised participation helped convince Wilson to commit American troops. He signed the authorization on June 1, 1918, and two months later American troops in England received notice that they were bound for Archangel. By then, the USS *Olympia*, patrolling the North Sea, had landed the first United States contingent of one hundred sailors and eight officers in Murmansk on June 8.

In 1918, Murmansk was a frontier port city of a couple thousand people in the extreme corner of northwestern Russia, only a few miles from Russia's borders with both Norway and Finland. Only two years old, its reason for being was that its harbor remained ice-free year-round due to the relatively warm waters of the North Atlantic Ocean current. As the only ice-free port in the Russian Arctic, it was the terminus for a hastily built railroad that provided a North Atlantic supply route to Russia during World War I. The Murmansk railroad stretched south along the Finnish border and around the White Sea, where it connected with other railroads to St. Petersburg. After the Treaty of Brest-Litovsk, German and Bolshevik troops had taken control of much of the railroad. Great Britain responded by sending its marines to keep Murmansk from falling into Bolshevik hands.

In early July, Bolshevik officials responded to the arrival of British marines by seizing and holding over two hundred British and French civilians and diplomats who were stationed in St. Petersburg. The American ambassador, David R. Francis, who was out of the city at the time, made his way north to Archangel, beyond the reach of the Bolsheviks, to await the arrival of the British and American troops. He waited about three weeks until British General Frederick Poole, commander of the Allied North Russia Expeditionary Force, stepped off the USS *Olympia* on August 3, at the head of 1,300 British and French soldiers and a small contingent of American sailors. An experienced military leader, Poole was a brusque, arrogant man who felt he deserved a better posting. Furthermore, he lacked any respect for the Russian people, a regrettable flaw that had unfortunate consequences for his military decisions and the men who implemented them.[10]

Because there were few Bolsheviks in the immediate area of Murmansk, the British soldiers and American sailors experienced no resistance — only curiosity — as they paraded into Archangel, led by the *Olympia*'s band. Bolshevik partisans had already fled the city by the time the *Olympia* appeared, and the soldiers and sailors soon boarded small boats and headed up the Dvina River in pursuit. They caught up with stragglers in a few days, and on August 15, 1918, a seaman, George Perschke, wounded while part of the pursuing force, became the first American casualty of the occupation.[11] As American sailors established their country's presence on Russian soil, Ambassador Francis

10. Willett, *Russian Sideshow*, pp. 5-10; Dennis Gordon, *Quartered in Hell: The Story of the American North Russia Expeditionary Force 1918-1919* (Missoula, MT: The Doughboy Historical Society, 1982), pp. 1-8.

11. Gordon, *Quartered in Hell*, p. 8.

awaited the arrival of the full 4,000-plus American contingent, which
was made up of the 339th Infantry Regiment, the 1st Battalion of the
310th Engineer Regiment, and the 337th Regiment's ambulance company and field hospital units.

It was at this point that Woodrow Wilson's decision to intervene
in Russia converged with Godfrey Anderson's military service. Anderson had been assigned to the 337th's hospital unit during basic training,
and now he and his comrades were headed for Russia. The selection of
the 339th Infantry and 337th Regiment's medical units came, in large
part, because they originated in Michigan and had experience with
harsh winters. In addition, their commander, Col. George Evan Stewart, had previously served in Alaska. Also significant was the fact that
their temporary location in England was Camp Aldershot, about
thirty-five miles southwest of London, and easily accessible by rail to
Newcastle, about 300 miles north, where they could board the troop
ships *Tydeus, Nagoya,* and *Somali* for their journey to Archangel.

By late August, the Americans were on their way to Russia. But it
was a star-crossed voyage from the beginning. No sooner had the ships
cleared Newcastle than Spanish flu broke out, and the members of the
hospital unit were set to work caring for the ill. To make matters
worse, medications that might have helped had remained in Newcastle,
set to follow on a later vessel. The first death of the expeditionary force
occurred during that transport of troops — not from enemy fire, but
from the invisible virus that had slipped onboard silently in England.
The burial took place at sea, not in the soon-to-be-established military
cemetery in Archangel. On September 4, after ten grueling days at sea,
the Americans arrived in Archangel, where the American sailors from
the *Olympia* and a contingent of 2,000 British, French, Serb, and Polish soldiers from infantry and artillery units awaited them.

It was a bedraggled and dispirited group of Americans, many of
them suffering from influenza, that stepped off the transport vessels.
Doctors sent the sickest directly to crowded makeshift hospital wards,
where thirty-five perished. The contagion they brought ashore quickly
spread to the local population, where it devastated the vulnerable Russians in Archangel, who lacked both resistance to the virus and ade-
quate medical care.

While the Americans recuperated from the influenza outbreak

and adjusted to their Archangel barracks, Colonel Stewart reported to Ambassador Francis. The latter, acting as President Wilson's representative in Archangel, reminded Stewart that the British General Poole, who had been developing a plan by which to deploy the new arrivals, was in command of the entire expedition. Poole planned his strategy around the two transportation routes that extended south from the port city: a railroad from Archangel to Vologda, and from there to Petrograd; and the Dvina River and its many branches, which, aided by a 130-mile railroad connection between the cities of Vologda and Yaroslava, transported the region's raw materials far to the south and east. With the onset of war, Archangel's importance and population had grown rapidly, and Poole was determined to keep it out of Bolshevik control. Although his expedition's stated mission was to guard the stockpiled supplies at Archangel, Poole set out to occupy the surrounding region as soon as he had sufficient manpower. Even before the arrival of the Americans, one group of his troops had pursued fleeing Bolsheviks down the railroad route toward Oberskaya, nearly 180 miles south of Archangel, while another pushed up the Dvina toward its junction with the Vaga River, 170 miles upriver.

When the Americans arrived, Poole divided them into two units and sent them to solidify the Allied force's hold on the two transportation routes. It was on the Dvina front, on September 16, 1918, that Pvt. Philip Sokol of Pittsburgh became the first American to die in combat action.[12] With its American reinforcements, the Dvina force pushed up the Vaga River an additional fifty miles beyond its junction with the Dvina to a small community named Shenkursk, where they rested briefly and then moved twenty miles further to several small villages, named Spasskoe, Sholosha, Nijni Gora, Visorka Gora, and Ust Padenga. The farther the Allied forces proceeded along the railroad — and up the Dvina and its tributaries — the more Bolshevik resistance they encountered.

Poole's Dvina front stretched hundreds of miles up the main river and its tributaries. The force penetrated a hundred miles east of Arch-

---

12. Joel R. Moore, Harry H. Mead, and Lewis E. Jahns, *The History of the American Expedition Fighting the Bolsheviki* (Detroit: Polar Bear Publishing Company, 1920), p. 300.

angel on the Pinega River and over two hundred miles south on the Vaga to Shenkursk. Further west, on the Murmansk Railroad front, troops held positions along the railroad from the port city to Kem, a distance of 350 miles, and on a parallel river route from the port of Onega south along a sixty-mile stretch of the Onega River. Poole's strategy had pushed the Bolsheviks from the Archangel region, but only temporarily. By the time the offensive halted, Poole's underestimation of the Bolshevik resistance had caused him to place his troops in a vulnerable position, with extended supply lines and a long perimeter that proved impossible to defend. Spread along a 450-mile front in the Russian forests and swamps, they settled in to build blockhouses, machine-gun nests, sentry posts, and barracks buildings that they expected to occupy during the long winter ahead.[13]

Back in Archangel, complaints from local leaders and the heads of the various international units, including the Americans, had convinced Poole's superiors in Great Britain to replace him with Major General Edmund Ironside, a more cautious tactician also known for his more engaging and diplomatic demeanor. Ironside took over in early November, at nearly the same moment that a negotiated armistice was bringing World War I combat to an end along the western front, leaving the intervention in Russia as the last active fighting of the war. Ironside was to reflect in his diary that advancing into the middle of Russia was "much as if one were pushing one's hand into a great sticky pudding [from which] one will never be able to extricate oneself."[14]

Even as the Allied troops struggled to establish a secure perimeter, they discovered to their chagrin that the Bolsheviks, skilled winter fighters who knew the topography and climate of the region, intended to fight through the winter. Bolshevik leaders stealthily moved men and artillery through the frozen swamps and forests to counteroffensive launching points, where they could wreak havoc on General Ironside's plan to pull his troops back cautiously. Instead, Bolshevik attacks forced speedy, disorganized retreats to positions near Archangel. At Shenkursk, where Godfrey Anderson's unit had established a small

13. Willett, *Russian Shideshow*, pp. 48-59, 75-112.
14. Gordon, *Quartered in Hell*, p. 9.

hospital for wounded soldiers, Bolshevik attackers nearly succeeded in encircling the entire Allied outpost. Only a remarkable nighttime re- treat along a seldom-used trail enabled them to avoid disaster. In his memoir, Anderson recalls packing severely wounded soldiers on sleighs pulled by Russian ponies, and he describes the horror of retreating from Shenkursk down forest trails through the long, dark Russian night.

The British decision to switch from offense to defense ultimately succeeded, but only after hundreds of Allied soldiers, including many Americans, lost their lives. Throughout that winter, General Ironside pulled his forces back into an increasingly tighter perimeter as Bolshevik fighters, constantly on the heels of the expeditionary force soldiers, attacked wherever they found vulnerable outposts. On more than one occasion, the Bolsheviks nearly encircled the withdrawing soldiers, and they did indeed inflict gruesome losses. In March 1919, when he was asked why his troops were fighting in Russia, Colonel Stewart did not speak about protecting military supplies or about car- rying out any other grand strategy, but said simply, "For their lives."[15] It was not until spring, nearly six months after the armistice had offi- cially ended the war, that the Americans and other members of the North Russia Expeditionary Force completed their retreat back to Archangel by boat, when the ice finally went out of Dvina Bay. Con- centrated around Archangel, the troops were defensively positioned to thwart further Bolshevik threats.

When World War I ended, much of the popular American support for sending troops to Russia ended with it, and as reports of the Bolshevik counteroffensive reached the West, Allied leaders came un- der increased pressure to end their Russian campaign. In Great Britain and the United States, sensational newspaper reports concerning the Bolshevik offensive and the Allied pullback intensified calls for troop withdrawal. When the *New York Times* reported that Shenkursk and nearby villages had fallen to Bolshevik counterattackers, calling it the beginning of a "North Russian offensive to drive invading forces into the sea," and that worried leaders in Archangel wanted reinforcements sent immediately, Republican Senator Hiram Johnson of California in-

---

15. Quoted in Dennis Gordon, *Quartered in Hell*, p. 10.

troduced a resolution calling on the government to withdraw all American troops from Russia. Subsequent reports told of Americans, Canadians, and British troops retreating "before [the] Reds in North Russia," and of Bolshevik artillery "shell[ing] our lines on the Vaga River."[16]

On February 10, the *Chicago Tribune* published a report declaring the Russian expedition a "pitiful failure" that had "failed to inspire confidence and loyalty and give real assistance to Russia," but instead had become "a cesspool of jealousy, hatreds, mistakes and shattered illusions." "From the start," wrote the *Tribune* correspondent, "the expedition lacked the thrill of the drive that a great, honest elated purpose would have given." As President Woodrow Wilson saw the tide of withdrawal sentiment rising, he concluded that it was time to end the ill-advised intervention. On February 18, 1919, he authorized Secretary of War Newton Baker to announce that he would withdraw American personnel "at the earliest possible moment that weather conditions in the spring will permit."[17]

To encourage the withdrawal, and to bolster the perception that the Allied occupation of the area was failing, Bolshevik leaders ordered a major drive against the Allied forces that paralleled the Onega River east of Archangel. At one point in early April, a Bolshevik force estimated at 7,000 attempted to drive a wedge between the expeditionary forces guarding the railroad and those on the Onega River; but they were repulsed. Thereafter, the Bolsheviks pulled back and waited for the Allied withdrawal to proceed. At the same time, Bolshevik propagandists sought to undermine troop morale by distributing leaflets that called on Allied soldiers to demand their return home now that the war with Germany was over.[18]

By mid-April, Godfrey Anderson and his fellow American sol-

16. "Reds Capture Shenkursk and Allies' Supplies," *New York Times,* Jan. 28, 1919; "Allies Again Fall Back before Reds in North Russia," *New York Times,* Feb. 2, 1919; "Reds Shell Our Lines on the Vaga River," *New York Times,* Feb. 8, 1919; "Assails Command in North Russia," *Chicago Tribune,* cited in *New York Times,* Feb. 10, 1919.

17. "Assails Command in North Russia," *New York Times,* Feb. 10, 1919; "Allies to Quit Archangel in Early Spring," *New York Times,* Feb. 18, 1919.

18. Willett, *Russian Sideshow,* pp. 5-9. Texts of Bolshevik leaflet examples can be found in Miles Hudson, *Intervention in Russia, 1918-1920: A Cautionary Tale* (South Yorkshire, England: Leo Cooper, 2005), pp. 188-90, 193-94.

In a downtown Archangel park, this British Mark V tank reminds current residents of the Allied troops that occupied the city in 1918-1920.　(http://en.wikipedia.org/wiki/archangelsk)

diers were back in Archangel or nearby, relieved in many cases by British soldiers who were brought in to take their place and whose leaders still believed they could thwart the spread of Bolshevism. As the new arrivals took over, the American Polar Bears assembled in a temporary embarkation camp for cursory medical examinations preparatory to their trip home. On June 3, 1919, they began boarding troop vessels and set off on their return to the United States, completing a journey that they had begun a year earlier. Initially sent to England, they had no notion they would be rerouted to a harsh winter in Russia, where at least nine officers and 213 men were casualties: 83 were killed in action; 27 later died of wounds; 69 died from diseases; 14 died from other causes; and 29 were reported missing in action.[19]

By all accounts, outside of the exemplary performances of the offi-

19. Sources give slightly differing numbers. I have used the compilation found in Moore et al., *The American Expedition*, pp. 299-303.

Archangel residents have not
forgotten the Allied intervention
of 1918. This monument honors
the "Defenders of the North,
1918-1920." (William C. Brumfield
Collection, Library of Congress, LC-
DIG-ppmsca-01234-DLC)

cers and soldiers, the North Russia Expeditionary Force had failed.
The undertaking began with a hazy, ill-defined mission, insufficient
materials and manpower, and an inconsistent strategy that left soldiers
deep in northern Russia's forests and swamps facing an angry foe who
had far better knowledge of the climate and terrain. Soldiers from
Great Britain and the other participating countries remained through
the summer, when they, too, departed. By November 1919, the entire
Allied North Russia Expeditionary Force was gone, and North Russia
was in the hands of its anti-Bolshevik government once again. That

government managed to hold on until February 1920, when it collapsed and its leaders fled.[20]

WHEN THEY RETURNED to the United States, most members of the
expeditionary force missed the excitement afforded soldiers who had
returned earlier. They went back to their peacetime pursuits and seldom talked about their sojourn in North Russia other than with other
veterans at reunions. Few in the United States today remember their
exploits. Only in Michigan, where a memorial association holds annual
commemorations and a Detroit cemetery features a symbolic "Polar
Bear" sculpture, has their service been honored.

That is not true among Russians, who recall the only American military force to set foot on Russian soil with bitterness. When Soviet pre-
mier Nikita Khrushchev visited the United States in 1959, he reminded
Americans of the expedition: "We remember the grim days when American soldiers went to our soil headed by their generals to help our White
Guard combat the new revolution. . . . All the capitalist countries of Europe and of America marched upon our country to strangle the new revolution. . . . Never have any of our soldiers been on American soil, but
your soldiers were on Russian soil. These are the facts."[21]

In Archangel today, a large monument reminds contemporary
Archangel residents of the "Defenders of the North," who battled the
Allied forces, resisting the expeditionary force. A captured British tank
on display in a downtown park reminds them of the time when foreign
troops occupied their city. There are other, less obvious reminders
throughout the region. Sections of abandoned railroads, destroyed
bridges, and decaying blockhouses remain as mute witnesses to the
conflict as the encroaching vegetation reclaims them. For those who
wish tangible proof of the bitter conflict that once battered this region
of northern Russia, Archangel researcher Alexy Suhanovsky maintains
a Web site where he displays photographs of both Allied and
Bolshevik blockhouses and trench ruins, military relics and remnants
that he has located, using his metal detector, at ruined military installa-
tions and battle sites.

20. Willett, *Russian Sideshow*, pp. 139-46.
21. E. M. Halliday, *When Hell Froze Over* (New York: IBooks, 2000), p. 305.

Armed with a metal detector, Archangel researcher Alexy Suhanovsky scours the country-side for remnants of 1918-1920 military action. Here he holds up a horseshoe he has discovered in the area. (http://pbma.grobel.org/ photos/alexy/photos_from_the_fronts .htm)

Russia's persistent recollection of that expedition and its combat suggests that her leaders have remembered the event better than have their counterparts in Great Britain and the United States. However, a look at the subsequent policies and military adventures of the nations involved suggests that neither side drew meaningful lessons concerning the perils of foreign military intervention from that ill-fated expedition.

CHAPTER ONE

From Farm Boy to Soldier

Godfrey Anderson was born in Sparta, Michigan, on November 14, 1895, the only child of Fred and Sophia Anderson, Swedish immigrants from the province of Smaland who had settled with several of their countrymen in and around this small farming community during the mid-1880s.[1] By the time their twenty-one-year-old son joined millions of other young Americans between the ages of twenty-one and thirty-one in the required registration for the initial draft shortly after the United States had officially entered World War I, on April 6, 1917, the Andersons had moved several times. Godfrey spent his first ten years in Sparta and attended its public schools. However, in 1905 his father, who worked as a cabinetmaker at the Welch Folding Bed Company factory in Sparta, decided to venture out on his own. Along with two of his brothers, Fred Anderson purchased a 100-acre farm near Murfreesboro, Tennessee, southeast of Nashville, and the three brothers moved their families to Tennessee. But a year later they decided that life in the South was not for them, and they returned to West Michigan. Fred was able to purchase a farm in eastern Ottawa County, near the community of Berlin.[2] That is where Godfrey Anderson grew to

1. Information about Godfrey Anderson's family and early life comes from an interview I conducted with him on January 22, 1981.

2. The town was named Berlin when Anderson graduated from high school and when he was drafted into the United States Army. But by the time he had returned

In Godfrey Anderson's youth, the commercial and governmental heart of Grand Rapids—and thus of West Michigan—was the intersection of Monroe Avenue and Pearl Street. On the left in this photo, looking southeast up Monroe, is the four-story Fifth National Bank Building, which was extended to ten stories in the mid-1920s, and later renamed McKay Tower. (Historic Photo Collection, Grand Rapids Public Library)

manhood: he finished his elementary education at the Kinney rural school and then enrolled at Berlin High School.

A diligent student and avid reader, Anderson especially enjoyed literature and history, and after spending three years at the small Berlin school, he decided to take advantage of the expanded programs at a larger school. In the fall of 1912 he transferred to Grand Rapids' Union High

from his tour of duty in World War I, the region's Congressman, Carl E. Mapes, had concluded that he did not want a Berlin in his district, and he acted to have the post office — and ultimately the town — change its name to Marne, which it remains to this day.

School, on the west bank of the Grand River, which had graduated its first senior class that spring. He also enjoyed sports, and though he was under-sized by modern standards, he joined Union's football team as a lineman. A serious injury, which he sustained when "a fifty-gallon fellow" fell on his leg in a game against the Grand Rapids powerhouse Central High School, ended his season as the team's center. By spring he had recovered suffi-ciently to play the outfield on a baseball team that won most of its games, including a victory over Central, which gave Godfrey a measure of satisfac-tion after his season-ending injury against that school the previous fall.

Anderson's formal schooling ended when he graduated from Union High School in the spring of 1913 and returned to work with his father on the family's Ottawa County farm. For the next five years he followed agri-culture's annual cycle, planting in the spring and caring for crops in the summer, harvesting them in the fall, all the while caring for cows, horses, and other animals. Young Godfrey's social life was focused on the youth group at the Swedish Mission Covenant Church in Grand Rapids, which re-mained his religious home throughout his life. With them he enjoyed church-sponsored activities, including group outings, Sunday school classes, and choir practice.

While tending to farm responsibilities and enjoying the camaraderie of his friends, Anderson, like nearly everyone else in America, watched war in Europe drag on relentlessly, destroying towns and cities and leaving mil-lions dead. Although hostilities had broken out in June 1914, the United States remained on the sidelines until almost three years later. In March 1917, the German decision to wage unconditional submarine warfare against U.S. merchant vessels, in addition to those of declared belligerents, caused President Woodrow Wilson to ask Congress for a dec-laration of war.[3]

3. The German western-front offensive, which began in late March 1918, was the plan of General Erich Ludendorff, who wanted to deliver a decisive blow to the Allies before American forces could be effectively deployed. The United States declared war on Germany on April 6, 1917, and troops began arriving in Europe in early 1918. Ger-many concluded the Treaty of Brest-Litovsk with Russia on March 3, 1918, and quickly began moving eastern front troops west. Although initially successful, the offensive produced heavy German casualties and stretched their supply lines; then it stalled when an estimated 250,000 American troops arrived. By summer's end, as American military might begin to make an impact, German leaders pursued a peace settlement.

This photo looks north from the intersection of Monroe Avenue and Pearl Street. On the left is the new Pantlind Hotel, which opened in 1915. Refurbished and renamed the Amway Grand Plaza in the 1980s, it remains a Grand Rapids landmark.
(Historic Photo Collection, Grand Rapids Public Library)

The national draft registration that accompanied the American war declaration changed the lives of young men across America.[4] Godfrey Anderson registered in early 1918; then, instead of returning to his father's

4. Over twenty-four million American men registered for military service under the terms of the Selective Service Act passed on May 18, 1917. The act established 52 state offices, one each for the 48 states, the District of Columbia, the territories of Alaska, Hawaii, and Puerto Rico; and 4,648 local draft boards to register and classify eligible males, determine their fitness, the order in which they were called, and to send them to training centers. During World War I, there were three registrations: on June 5, 1917, for all men between the ages of 21 and 31; on June 5, 1918, for those who attained age 21 after June 5, 1917; and on September 12, 1918, for men aged 18 through 45.

farm, he found a position with the Baldwin, Tuthill and Bolton Company of Grand Rapids, makers of band, blade, and circular saws and other tools for the lumbering and furniture industries. He went to live at the home of a family friend, Gust Aspergren, from which he could walk a short distance to work every day. Three months after he had begun his job at the factory, a letter from his local draft board ended his employment and any apprehensiveness he might have had about when — or if — he would be called up for military service.

A few days after he received his induction notice, Godfrey was on his way to Fort Custer, near Battle Creek, Michigan, for basic training with the U.S. Army's 85th Division, which was made up of inductees from Michigan and Wisconsin. After completing training, the new draftees were to ship out to England. Godfrey was only beginning his basic training as a soldier; he had no way of knowing that a decision already made by President Wilson had sealed his fate. He and fellow members of the 337th Regiment's hospital unit would eventually find themselves struggling to survive a harsh Russian winter as part of the North Russia Expeditionary Force. It was an adventure that affected the young farm boy so profoundly that he felt compelled to write his memoir of the experience.

"Toward an uncertain future . . ."

It was the 21st of March 1918 that the German army launched its great spring offensive. I remember the big black headlines in the papers as the seemingly irresistible force swept forward day after day. That was about the time when I went down to Grand Haven on the Muskegon interurban to register for the draft.[1] It was a grey gloomy rainy day and

1. The Grand Rapids, Grand Haven and Muskegon light railway line, a subsidiary of the Westinghouse Electric & Manufacturing Company, operated from 1902 to 1928 between Grand Rapids and Muskegon. A branch line ran from Fruitport, about five miles southeast of Muskegon, to Grand Haven, where the line offered a Lake Michi-

it seemed we had to hang around the courthouse most of the day, which was a good preview of what the army was to be. I remember I went out around noon and took a walk out to the pier and viewed the bleak prospect along the Lake Michigan Shore. Later that afternoon the medical examiner finally got thru working me over and I managed to get home in time for supper. At that time we lived at the extreme east end of Ottawa County on what is now called Johnson St. [Three Mile Road NW in Kent County], 3/4 of a mile west of the Kent-Ottawa Co. line where the G.R., G.H., & Muskegon interurban crossed the road.

In the meantime I had gotten a job at the Baldwin, Tuthill & Bolton Machine Shop in G.R. and was boarding over at Gust Aspegren's home on Third St.[2] It was about the middle of May when I got a notice to report for induction into the army. I resigned my job the week before and took what might be called a preliminary vacation. I had just got engaged at that time and it was something of a romantic interlude. Between times I remember lying down by a sunny window upstairs and reading with pleasure an ancient copy of Cervantes' "Don Quixote" with the Doré illustrations.[3] One night the Walker Sunday School had a surprise party for me and gave me a kit of toilet and other articles for camp use.

I was ordered to report on the day before Decoration Day, [May 29] 1918.[4] My father drove me down to the little green waiting station

---

gan boat connection to Chicago. The Coopersville Area Historical Museum maintains one of the railway's original substations and a restored passenger car.

2. Anderson's room at the Aspergrens' home was only about six blocks from his job at Baldwin, Tuthill and Bolton, which was located at 505 Sixth Street. *Directory for Grand Rapids, Michigan* (Detroit: R. L. Polk Co., 1917).

3. French artist Gustave Doré (1832-1883) illustrated over 200 books, some with more than 400 plates, in his lifetime. He is primarily known for his illustrations of *Paradise Lost, The Divine Comedy, Don Quixote*, and Edgar Allan Poe's "The Raven." He also produced hundreds of Bible story illustrations.

4. Communities began observing Decoration Day immediately after the Civil War. Waterloo, New York, is credited with being the holiday's official birthplace because it observed the day on May 5, 1866 (established as May 30 in 1868). Congress officially declared it Memorial Day in 1967, and a year later passed the Uniform Holidays Bill, which moved Washington's birthday (now President's Day), Veterans Day, and Memorial Day to specified Mondays in order to create three-day holiday weekends.

at the county line, where I got aboard the 8:00 interurban. That interurban was operated by means of a third rail. On freezing wintry days you could see the flares as the shoes bounced over the third rail as far as Nunica, creating flashes like some animated Aurora Borealis. The car's first stop was at Berlin (later called Marne) where Bert Blink, who ran the feed store/lumber yard there, and Bert Walcott, an old schoolmate and fellow player on the Berlin High School baseball team got aboard, they also being inducted that day. It was a pleasant morning, cool and delightful as May always is at that time of the year. We got off at the street in Grand Haven where the Armory was a couple of blocks to the south.

Baldwin, Tuthill & Bolton was a small Grand Rapids manufacturer of saws, drills, grinders, and related tools for the furniture industry when Godfrey Anderson went to work for them in 1918. (Baldwin, Tuthill & Bolton Manual, 1920, p. 295)

There was a good sized crowd there milling around keeping tabs on their suitcases and gripsacks. I noticed one raw-boned farmer in overalls who had his belongings stored in a gunny sack. There were a number of civilians on hand, friends, relatives and curious onlookers, and there was a long string of cars parked in the area. Presently an official of some kind appeared on the scene and began checking off a list, along with an informal roll call, a pep talk, and various instructions. Presently the line of cars drew abreast one by one and each picked up three or four of the inductees lined up in front of the armory, until all had found a place. Then the procession of cars turned up the flag bedecked main street, forming a sort of parade with people on the sidewalks waving and calling to us. The cavalcade moved past the park and the court house and presently turned south along the highway — headed for Holland. After passing the city limits it picked up speed and continued on alongside the railroad on the right. About half an hour later the procession stopped, for what reason I do not know unless it was for the consideration of the passengers, who at any rate climbed out and without more ado relieved themselves behind the bushes that lined the road.

We pulled up in the main street of Holland around noon and were headed up into some large public hall, where tables were lined up and a nice luncheon set out for each of us, with friendly ladies in attendance. We were regaled with patriotic speeches from some of the county offi-

Grand Rapids' Bridge Street bridge was the city's primary East Side–West Side crossing point at the beginning of the twentieth century. In this view, the Grand Rapids–Muskegon Interurban Depot is on the left at the river, and the Grand Rapids Brewing Company building is on the right looking east, up Michigan Street hill.   (Postcard Collection, Grand Rapids Public Library)

cials and the District Congressman, Dykema or Dyman if I remember right.[5]

After the inner man had been appeased and our egos inflated by the pep talks and flowery phrases, we were herded down the street to the depot where a locomotive and train of cars stood waiting. We piled aboard and accommodated ourselves as best we could with our luggage, and after the usual delay we were off headed for Grand Rapids.

We pulled into the Union Depot there in the latter part of the afternoon.[6] The next we knew we marched in twos up Ionia Avenue and

5. Republican Gerrit J. Diekema represented the area in the U.S. Congress from 1908 to 1911. He was highly regarded for his oratorical skills. William Schrier, *Gerrit J. Diekema, Orator: A Rhetorical Study of the Political and Occasional Addresses of Gerrit J. Diekema* (Grand Rapids: Eerdmans, 1950); C. Warren Vander Hill, *Gerrit J. Diekema* (Grand Rapids: Eerdmans, 1970).

6. Built in 1900, Union Depot, with massive columns at its entrance and a large

Grand Rapids' Union Railroad Depot was West Michigan's transportation hub. It was the last place Godfrey Anderson and soldiers like him saw as they left home, and the first place they saw upon their return.   (Postcard Collection, Grand Rapids Public Library)

wound up at the Majestic Theatre.[7] We all went in and took seats to view a movie, then in progress. What the movie was I don't remember, if I ever did find out. Anyway we didn't get to see the end of it, for before that we were unceremoniously ordered out again and retraced our steps back to the train, a rather bedraggled looking outfit it must have appeared to the spectators on the streets.

When we climbed in the coaches parked in the tracks behind the

---

two-story lobby, served as the railroad gateway to West Michigan until it was destroyed in 1961 to make way for a U.S. 131 off-ramp to downtown Grand Rapids. Its site is now occupied by a parking lot for the Van Andel Arena.

7. Opened in 1903 at the corner of Library and Division as a vaudeville theater, the Majestic became a movie house as motion pictures grew in popularity and supplanted live acts. The theater became home to the Grand Rapids Civic Theatre in 1979. A grant from the Meijer Foundation funded a $10 million renovation that was completed in 2006, when the theater was renamed the Meijer Majestic Theatre, part of the Grand Rapids Civic Theatre and School of Theatre Arts complex.

depot we found that some kind hearted organization had placed wrapped lunches on all the seats to which we did ample justice. The time now was late afternoon or early evening and there were a number of curious people loitering about, especially a number of young females who waved to us enthusiastically as the train began to slowly move out of the station and headed south. There was a certain letdown, a certain sense of misgiving as the shadows began to fall and the sun was inclining to the west and as our homes began to recede behind us and we moved toward an uncertain future. After an hour or so we began to approach our destination, which had been named Camp Custer, after that famous Michigander, Civil War veteran and Indian fighter General George Armstrong Custer.[8]

We just caught sight of those tall, black chimneys rising in stacks of four at intervals along the route. The camp seemed to extend for miles — a veritable city of barracks. The train finally halted at the north end where we disembarked at what was called, I believe, the Depot Brigade. This was a large raw-looking unpainted building, as were the hundreds of barracks and other buildings stretching off in all directions. Here we sat or lounged about for an eternity it seemed, with night beginning to fall. Presently a ragged line was established, and each of us entered the building and each was handed a blanket roll in which was tucked various articles including an aluminum mess kit holding a knife, fork and spoon with a cover snapped on and a folding cup. After receiving this we returned to our former location out front and resumed our endless vigil, listening to the variety of sounds both near and afar, the sounds of traffic, motor busses, of bugles far off, a

8. Camp Custer was established as a training facility in July 1917; its first draftees reported in September of that year. It was designated a demobilization center after the war, and the Veterans Bureau established the Battle Creek Veterans Hospital at the site in the early 1920s. Renamed Fort Custer in 1940, it became a permanent military base at which more than 300,000 World War II soldiers trained; it also housed 5,000 German prisoners of war during that war. Secretary of Defense Robert McNamara ordered Fort Custer's closing in 1964. Since 1968, Michigan has used a portion of the reserve for National Guard training, while another portion is now a state park and recreation area. The most dramatic Fort Custer change is the portion designated Fort Custer Industrial Park, which has attracted more than ninety companies and created an estimated 9,000 jobs.

constant subdued undercurrent of sound along with the chirping of crickets and night insects.

Along toward midnight, it seemed some gravel-voiced non-coms appeared and roughly lined us up in a column of twos extending about a hundred yards, and started us off. There was a wide roadway running through the center of the camp from end to end. This was dimly lighted and visibility left much to the imagination. We stumbled along like robots in a fog, dead tired, carrying suitcases in one hand and the bedroll over our shoulders. Now and then someone's mess kit fell out scattering the lid and contents helter-skelter in the darkness. There would be a string of curses by the owner and some rude guffaws from his amused compatriots.

Once they arrived in Battle Creek, new draftees marched from the railroad depot to Camp Custer to begin their U.S. Army basic training.
(Willard Library Historical Photographs Collection)

A bit later this rookie cavalcade was ordered to halt and the rear half of the line was marched off toward a cluster of barracks to the left. It was long after lights-out and the area seemed largely deserted, dark and quiet. We found out later that this half of our group had been diverted over to the infantry section. It was all indiscriminate; we had fallen into line in a haphazard manner and those who chanced to fall into the lower half of the line were destined for the trenches. It so happened that both Bert Blink and Bert Walcott had found themselves in this tail end category. In fact I had seen little of either during that hectic day. And so, due to blind chance, as it were, Blink would lose an eye and Walcott a leg somewhere over in Argonne later that summer. The remaining segment of the file stumbled on for nearly a mile or so until we were halted in front of an empty barracks off to one side and were herded up a stairway at one end to the second floor, all one large undivided space with a row of windows and a line of cots along each side. We were instructed to pick a cot at random and hit the alfalfa, which we did, needing no second invitation, after which the lights were turned off. It had been a long grueling day and everyone was dog tired. I for one crawled under the newly issued blanket and into the waiting arms of Morpheus and fell into dreamless oblivion.

We were rudely awakened next morning by the blast of the reveille bugle next door, a ritual that seemed to be taking place all over the camp. There was a yelping and barking and as we looked out the window we saw the neighboring outfit lined up undergoing roll call. I had somehow gotten a bunk between the two Boelens brothers from Spring Lake, Gary and Herman, and for some reason, they were convulsed in laughter, having found something ludicrous in their present situation. We quickly got acquainted, and began looking over the other recruits, all strangers, who were stirring about with various comments and reactions. It seemed we were in the charge of a young corporal, who soon put in an appearance and marshaled us over to a dining hall where we were served a good breakfast at one of the long tables running the length of the room.

It was Decoration Day; the weather was lovely. It was a sort of holiday in the camp too. Many were away on leave, yet the place had the appearance of a gigantic ant hill. All along to the east of the main highway that bisected the camp were extensive parade grounds, for drilling and maneuvers, all dusty and denuded of grass by incessant tramping but there was no drilling there today, it being a holiday. Off to the west ran a busy public highway, today the traffic having more of a holiday aspect. We soon located the washroom, toilet and latrine allocated to us. We noticed two special seats reserved for "Generals" only. We discovered the recreation rooms, the Y.M.C.A., the commissary, the theatre, auditorium, Red Cross and various other points of interest in our immediate vicinity — places where there were newspapers, magazines, free writing paper and envelopes.

On a holiday such as this, as well as on Sundays, a host of visitors invaded the camp coming by bus, automobiles, interurbans, excursion trams or other means, and the area would be full of sightseers — ladies in gay dress escorted by gentlemen in their Sunday best — parents, relatives, friends and a legion of the curious, and the place took on the character of some extravagant exposition or state fair. The most impressive moment of the day for these visitors was at sunset when the troops all over the camp stood at attention in front of their barracks, amid the bugle calls, while the bands played the national anthem and the flags came down, as regulations demanded.

It was a day of activity and excitement for us green recruits, and we especially appreciated the generous and good food served, the holiday and Sunday menus being a bit extra with ice cream and chicken, etc.

Some of our outfit spent the afternoon exploring and sightseeing, some visiting canteens, some relaxing, smoking cigarettes, or playing poker; I myself got involved in a ball game in the hollow below the barracks.

But the next day and the days following there was considerable activity. Nearly every day it was to retrace our steps along those long treks up toward the other end of the camp, now to pick up our O.D. uniforms (the non-com in charge merely sized us up and tossed us a blouse, shirt and pair of trousers all by guess and by golly).[9] Some time we went up to get our shoes heavy and ponderous, or maybe it would be underwear, knapsacks, socks or a poncho, shelter half with stakes and poles, or felt campaign hats with a cord around the rim of a certain color designating the particular branch of the service the wearer belonged to. Every day it seemed we plodded up that same dusty trail, to get a shot for each of a variety of diseases, and the grinning vets along the way would give us cat calls and holler, "Wait till you get that second shot, oh boy!" However, their barking was much worse than the actual bite. One time we had to go through another general physical examination similar to the one we had before being inducted into the army. A few failed to pass this time and were discharged, not too happily, there being a certain humiliation and inferiority complex involved.

A bit later, having finally got most of our equipment and uniforms we were lined up for our first drill in charge of a red headed foul-mouthed sergeant. He began by delivering a violent diatribe consisting mostly of threats, cussing, and obscenities, his voice at times rising almost to a shriek as he belabored us with vituperation and insult, referring to us repeatedly as bastards and sons of bitches. Whether all that was some form of army psychology, devised to intimidate new recruits and put them in a proper subservient frame of mind, I never knew. What seemed incomprehensible was that an officer — a lieutenant — stood right behind him, impassive and preoccupied, making no slightest effort to temper this vile ranting. We went through the rudimentary formations, marching by fours, turning obliquely or at right angles,

9. Wool olive drab uniforms were adopted in 1902 for use by soldiers in the field. A blue dress uniform served for ceremonies and off-post wear. (Stephen J. Kennedy, "The Army Dressed Up," *Quartermaster Review,* Jan./Feb. 1952.)

reversing to the rear, etc., along with a variety of calisthenics, all under a barrage of scathing abuse. This drilling went on for several days under the direction of this same nasty martinet. However, one hot, blistering day one of the recruits keeled over and lay dead to the world in the dust. He soon revived, but the ranting suddenly ceased; the officers seemed disconcerted and a bit apprehensive, and the outfit was summarily dismissed for the day. That was the last we saw of that particular sergeant.

Sometimes we were taken to lectures on venereal diseases and saw on a screen some horrible pictures of the various aspects of syphilis, [?] chancres and the like. The regulations we learned required that any soldier exposed to a venereal disease must submit to an immediate prophylactic treatment. If he did so, but nevertheless acquired the disease he suffered no further penalty; if not he was indeed in bad shape. We soon discovered other forms of entertainment in the evenings: movies, band concerts, the Battle Creek Symphony. Sometimes we took trips to Battle Creek nearby; the streets there were jammed with men in uniform constantly compelled to salute officers every few feet, who in turn must have been heartily sick of and exasperated at having to return those continual and interminable salutes.

After some two or three weeks I, among others, got my first weekend pass. Shortly after the dinner mess we on leave hoofed it up to the north end of the camp where the trains and interurban stations were. The day was radiant and we who were headed north clambered aboard the olive-green Grand Rapids & Kalamazoo interurban parked there.

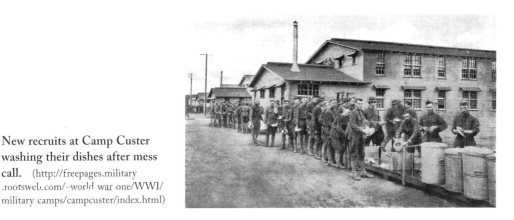

New recruits at Camp Custer washing their dishes after mess call. (http://freepages.military .rootsweb.com/~world war one/WWI/ military camps/campcuster/index.html)

In due time we pulled out, all in high spirits and keen anticipation. However we had not gone much farther than the Gull Lake area when something went wrong with the mechanism and the car became stalled. We thought little of it at the time, a momentary inconvenience, we believed soon to be rectified. But time passed and no relief appeared. Men became impatient; an hour passed, some who lived farther north would miss their train connections in Grand Rapids. Some of the men milled about, cursing and angry, and an ugly situation was developing. It was considerably later that a replacement arrived on the scene and the disgruntled passengers resumed their journey. Now a spirit of vengeful vandalism soon began to manifest itself; every loose object, or what could be wrenched loose, cuspidors, curtains, mats went out the windows, rolls of toilet paper, rotated outside around sticks, sent streamers traveling far to the rear. The motorman and conductor up front discreetly made no remonstrance nor attempt to interfere. We finally arrived in Grand Rapids way overdue and some of those headed further north did indeed miss their connections. For me it was a comparatively small inconvenience. The Muskegon interurban terminal was over on Ottawa St. in front of their depot in the Houseman Building (now razed) and a car left on every hour.[10] Needless to say I was happy to see the old folks at home, and vice versa. I spent most of my time with my best girl, driving around in the old Model T, and got back to camp late Sunday night.

Shortly after this our outfit of greenhorn neophytes was split up. We had received most of our equipment, our "shots," and the preliminary training and drilling. Some of us, including the Boelens brothers and another native of Spring Lake, one Fred Beard, were transferred over to the 337th field hospital unit, occupying a barracks a short distance farther south. This was a much larger place, with kitchen, dining hall, lavatory and latrines. Here we got acquainted with a new set of characters, who were to be our comrades, or unit, for the rest of our military careers. The 337th was part of the 310th Sanitary Train, under command of Major Jonas Longely, of Fond-du-Lac, Wisc., along with

---

10. The Houseman Building, built by former Grand Rapids mayor Julius Houseman between 1883 and 1886, stood on the north side of Ottawa Avenue between Pearl and Lyon streets.

Captains Kinyon, Martin, Lieuts. Cote, Danzinger, Lowenstein. The top sergeants were Mattson, Walters and a number of other sergeants and corporals, Harter, Parden, Andrews, Bates, Thornton, to mention a few.

Our daily drills and calisthenics were now resumed in earnest. We were lined up in order of height beginning at the left, which established the order of our permanent lineup. The five tallest were Kenderson, Sneburger, Rhinehart, Whitmore, Carnes (I was no. 6). We were roused at six in the morning by the blast of Pvt. Coleman's bugle. Then the morning roll call, the chow, the washing, the shaving and making up our bunks and reclining thereon, smoking cigarettes until the peremptory bark from below ordered us out for the morning drills. There was more lounging and relaxing before and after the noon rations call, then the same routine was pursued in the afternoon until chow time and the evening roll call. Between times there was K.P. — peeling great piles of potatoes, sweeping and dusting and policing the grounds. For relaxation between times there was the reading of novels, writing letters, shooting craps or playing poker; some had mandolins, mouth organs, ukuleles, etc. The air was thick with tobacco smoke, and the noisy conversation on all sides consisted largely of profanity, four letter words, vituperation, cussing of the army, and obscenity in general.

Most every morning we would set off on a hike, past the artillery regiment located beyond a wide ravine or hollow to the south of us, then farther out past the base hospital at the extreme end of the camp, then on through the flowering woodlands lovely beyond compare as they always are in June. At last we came to the Kalamazoo River which we crossed on a red iron truss bridge and entered the town of Augusta, our hobnails clattering on the paved street. Coming back the company would usually go through its repertoire of ribald songs, the favorites being: "Bang Away at Lulu" and "The Old Gray Mare Ain't What She Used To Be," etc.

As said before those extensive training fields running alongside the camp were long since denuded of grass by thousands of tramping feet that had ground up a layer of black dust. On windy days there would be a dust storm, which penetrated everywhere, got in the bunks and even the food, befouling and dirtying everything.

The personnel of the 337th, which called for 50 [?] enlisted men, was

Camp Custer trainees enjoyed social functions such as this dance, to which young women from the surrounding communities were invited.
(Willard Library Historical Photographs Collection)

not yet complete, requiring some additional draftees to bring its enrollment up to par. One day this quota arrived, recruits mostly from the Chicago area, of Slavic backgrounds, largely Polish, Lithuanian, with some Balkan, Italian and Jewish thrown in. There being no accommodations available in the barracks just then, this crew was quartered in pup tents in the hollow a little below the 337th barracks. One night in late June a terrific thunderstorm came up with a deluge of rain, which continued all night long. In the morning when we looked out the window we saw that the valley was flooded and looked like a miniature pond, all the pup tents were down and floating around and the recruits were wading around bedraggled and forlorn trying to salvage their belongings. They were eventually dried out and more or less rehabilitated.

During the latter part of the month of June the company began taking those all-day hikes. We would set out in the morning marching in columns of fours and heading off for some lake out in the country. We would drop out a couple of times for a short rest before reaching our destination. Arriving there we would open our knapsacks, devour our rations, and relax awhile, enjoying the scenery around the lake. We would arrive back in camp in late afternoon, dead tired. I remember once we took a longer, tougher all-day hike the day before the 4th of July. Coming back, some dropped out, utterly exhausted and the truck had to come and pick them up. One bad feature of these hikes was this: the foursome up front were the tallest and strongest and they walked along in uncontaminated air, kicking up a cloud of dust which made the breathing especially tough for the smaller, lighter men bringing up the rear, sweating in the heat under their heavy packs and breathing polluted air. The officers were a bit concerned that night for they examined all our feet looking for blisters. For my part I was used to long hikes afoot in the country and suffered no foot sores. In fact I had to hoof it two miles to high school in Berlin through unbroken snowdrifts two feet deep in winter for four years. I had a pass back to G.R. over the 4th and was out late that night. I was so tired that I spent most of the day home on the couch instead of going to the Sunday School picnic as I had planned.

At one time there was the so-called gas mask training. There was a building filled with gas and we put on our masks and entered and milled about a bit then came out without any incident or effects. There were a few times when we had what might be called educational sessions down in the hollow under a tremendous oak tree. Once it was to teach us the names of all the bones in the body — occipital, clavicle, femur, etc. — another time there were demonstrations of wrapping, bandaging, and other practical tips of value to a medical corps, as we were. At another time one of the officers undertook to teach us something of French, at least a sample vocabulary. "What do they call potatoes in French?" the officer slyly asked George Whitmore. George was a tall tow-headed farmer, a simple-minded fellow, not quite all there mentally, but physically capable. "They call them Murphys down where I come from," he mumbled. It was at one of these sessions that a bird parked in the foliage above, released what might be termed an explosive bomb, which landed with a lush, odoriferous splash squarely on the shoulder of the officer's dress uniform.

It was around the 11th of July that we took our first and, as events

Along with all other recruits, Godfrey Anderson received gas mask training. Mustard gas was a feared World War I weapon that either killed its victims or left their lungs scarred for life. (Willard Library Historical Photographs Collection)

turned out, our last overnight hike. We started out in the morning right after reveille on a pleasant but potentially hot day. We headed north this time and in due time were clattering through the outskirts of Battle Creek. Presently we were out in the country, tramping along dirt roads which we followed until noon when we fell out and flopped down at a pleasant roadside spot, where we made the most of the rations we carried in our knapsacks and condiment cans. I, for myself, was sound asleep when the march began an hour or so later. We tramped all afternoon along the dusty country roads, past corn fields and apple orchards, and golden wheat fields ripe for cutting, past ancient homesteads and here and there dilapidated barns.

It was late in the afternoon when we reached our destination: a hillside on the north side of Lake St. Mary's, which sloped gently down to the water's edge.[11] For the last hour or two the outfit had slogged along too tired even to bawl out those bawdy songs they had chanted so lustily earlier in the day. We staked out our pup tents in a haphazard attempt at geometrical precision. Each pup tent accommodated two persons; each soldier carried what was called a shelter half with stakes and poles, and two of these were hooked together to make a tent. There was some kind of a chow prepared, a roll call and check off and an order to fall out was issued. In the area back by the road were places where one could purchase cigarettes, candy bars and ice cream. Off in the west the sun was setting in a blaze of amber glow. The foot end of the tents faced the lake with its shimmering reflections, the peeping of small night creatures, the chirping of insects and the deep croaking of bullfrogs. Presently a full moon began rising grandly in the east, and all above the heavens were studded with glittering stars. All at once the mournful notes of the bugler playing taps broke the silence of the night. My partner, one Van Sickle, and I slept on that hard ground throughout that night without waking once.

We were rudely awakened next morning by the brassy blast of a bugle. There were even ruder and more peremptory blasts as those Caligula-dispositioned top sergeants snarled curt commands to "snap out of it." A sudden order had come through from Headquarters. The

---

11. St. Mary's Lake is about seven miles northeast of Camp Custer and two miles north of Battle Creek.

85th was moving out. Tonight! We hurriedly dismantled the pup tents, rolled our packs and bolted something in the way of breakfast. The sun was already up off to our left and the sky was a robin's egg blue, cloudless and serene. We now moved off at a much faster clip than the day before, not on the same route as we traveled yesterday but taking direct short cuts over dirt side roads. There were no fallings-out now, no rest periods this time and the sweaty bedraggled columns reached the home barracks some time after noon, having returned in nearly half the time it took to make the outgoing journey the day before.

From then on the afternoon was one of feverish activity, the packing and cleaning up, and a barrage of conflicting orders, the pushing of trunks, boxes, barracks bags and supplies in carts over to the railroad tracks where row upon row of railroad coaches were waiting. We loaded our baggage in a string of cars labeled "Lehigh Valley." The whole camp as far as we could see was in a similar upheaval and uproar. It was then that the first realization and implication of what was going on finally dawned upon us. The 85th Division was headed for the war zones. I had little conception where the Lehigh Valley was, off in the Appalachian area somewheres, I surmised. Finally toward evening we lined up for a final inspection and roll call. It was at that moment one Pvt. Paul Shepard, who had overstayed his leave showed up, just in the nick of time, but the ominous scowl of the officers was not at all reassuring.

It was somewhere between 7 and 8 o'clock when we bid farewell for the last time to the old barracks, and began our trek down to the railroad sidings where the trains were waiting. I and some others had been in service not quite six weeks. We recruits were now in the medical corps, the Field Hospital, but we had received practically no training during that time, and had little idea what our duties were to be. About all the training we had received was largely in discipline and drilling and being put in good physical condition, in which, indeed we were. At any rate we clambered aboard the coaches with our cumbersome packs and took seats and stowed our luggage as best we could. Then the endless wait, as usual, trying to relax amid the usual clouds of cigarette smoke creating a blue haze. Finally, at long last, there was the clanging of bells, the hissing of escaping steam and gradually the cars began to move. Slowly we passed the seemingly endless profusion of the unpainted raw barracks, the various power houses with their quadruple smokestacks and the vast beehive that was Camp Custer.

Finally we hit the main tracks of the Michigan Central Railroad and headed east at an increased speed. The evenings are long at that time of the year and visibility was still good when we passed through Jackson. Night had not quite fallen as we bisected Ann Arbor nor yet at Ypsilanti, but when we hit the outposts of Detroit it was amid descending gloom. We were a long time passing through that metropolitan jungle; with a million lights flashing by amid a tremendous clattering of rails, but at long last we pulled into the Union Depot there. After the usual delay, we again got underway at a reduced speed, and presently with a roar we entered the tunnel beneath the Detroit River and after a monotonous din we emerged at Windsor, and continued on into Canada. It was all pitch black outside now, and I tried to adjust myself to the cramped position I was in and tried to get some sleep.

I did doze off fitfully, as it were, snatching a few winks now and then, but too frequently aroused by the heaving and rolling of the cars, the incessant clattering, and the unearthly scream of the whistle up front to get any real rest during that night.

I was jarred awake for the last time, and became aware that it was daylight outside. Somehow the long night had passed. Some of my companions were already stirring about, wondering just where we were in that lower promontory of Ontario. Not long after we found out. We were passing thru a town called Niagara Falls. With keen anticipation we kept eyes glued to the windows and presently the train began crossing the International Bridge across the Niagara River. In the gorge below the water was heaving and tossing in the wildest turbulence. Looking upstream the Falls were completely obscured by a cloud of white mist rising high above it. Over on the other side we crossed the old Erie Canal somewhere around Tonawanda. At the Buffalo outskirts the milk wagons were making their rounds, along with men carrying dinner pails on their way to work. Somewhere in this area we transferred to the Lehigh Valley tracks and headed straight east for Batavia, some thirty miles distant. Somewhere along mid morning we stopped at a town called Geneva. Here we gratefully received refreshment from some local organization. A little beyond Geneva the railroad took a right angled turn to the south. Here the route continued along the east shore of one of those Finger Lakes — Seneca it was. The scenery was entrancingly beautiful. The lake was at most only a mile wide, scarcely wider than the lower Mississippi beyond St. Louis, and the various fields and farmlands checkered in various patches of green, yellow and gold rose from the opposite shore to the distant horizon. Lake Seneca extends some thirty-five miles from Geneva to its southern end to Watkins Glen, a delightful vista all the way. About thirty-five miles further on, after curving off [to] the southeast, through a series of low foothills, the train came to a halt at Sayre [Pennsylvania], just over the New York–Pennsylvania state line. Here the Susquehanna River comes in from the E./N. E. and curves in a wide semicircle of more than a twenty mile radius then heads off to the S and S. E.

At Sayre the 337th was ordered outside and, marching by fours, took a swing around the environs of the town to loosen up the stiff joints. Our Corporal Harter claimed Sayre was his home town. We reboarded the train in the early part of the afternoon and resumed our journey. Now the terrain took on a much different aspect. The foothills loomed higher and higher on both sides and presently became towering hills or mountains but thickly wooded to the very crests. The river wound in a serpentine course thru the gorge it had cut during past geologic ages. The railroad crossed to the east side of the river at Towanda, where the river begins a long series of tortuous loops and convolutions, and tracks following the narrow space between the river and the base of the mountains. All afternoon the train, its whistle screaming eerily to the high heavens, wound and twisted its way thru the sunless abyss below the towering heights.

Later that afternoon the river and track straightened out somewhat and took a turn to the S.W. About 15 miles below this turn the train came to a stop at historic Wilkes-Barre, a city of some 75,000 inhabitants. Here the 337th detrained again and were escorted over to the Y.M.C.A. for a welcome snack and a bit of relaxation. In the train yards we noticed some WAACS in overalls greasing and oiling locomotives.[12] After we returned to our places in the coaches there was a

12. Anderson is wrong in assuming that the women he saw were members of the Women's Army Auxiliary Corps, or WAAC, which was not organized until the beginning of World War II. In World War I, 13,000 women enlisted in the U.S. Navy,

bit of delay before the train got underway. Quite a crowd had assembled, including a number of young ladies, and there was an animated flirtation between the loquacious doughboys leaning out of the windows and the pretty girls giggling below. The sun was swinging low behind the purple hills in the west, and as the train finally began to pull out there were cries of farewell and cheers, a great waving of hands and blowing of kisses.

From then on I have no idea of the route we took. I had not slept well the night before and was dead tired. Determined to get a better night's rest I flopped on the floor between the seats with legs protruding out in the aisle. I noticed my equally tired companions made similar arrangements as best they could.

For my part I slept like a log the entire night. When I was rudely awakened next morning I found we were parked on a side track with innumerable rows of boxcars on each side completely obstructing any view. Here the entire company was assembled under the vicious snarls of the top sergeant and presently we were tramping over the cinders between the long strings of boxcars and finally entered and passed through a building, and on to what proved to be the deck of a ferry-boat. I for one had no idea where we were until we came out into the open at the front deck. Then to my astonishment there across the Hudson loomed Manhattan — lower N. Y. City thickly congested with towers and skyscrapers, stretching off in the distance as far as the eye could reach. There was an endless profusion of piers on both sides of the river, on which all manner of tugs, ferries and shipping were darting about with continued activity like restless terriers. I, for my part, stood completely dumbfounded, gaping spellbound at the magnificent scene. It seems we were somewhere in Jersey City about oppo-

---

mostly doing clerical work. They were the first women in U.S. history to be admitted to full military rank and status. The U.S. Army hired women nurses and telephone operators to work overseas, but as uniformed civilian employees. Plans for a World War I women's auxiliary corps (in which they would perform mostly clerical, supply, and communications work) were shot down by the war department, as were plans for commissioning women doctors in the medical corps. The end of the war brought an end to proposals to enlist women in the army for another two decades. Joshua S. Goldstein, *War and Gender: How Gender Shapes the War System and Vice Versa* (Cambridge: Cambridge University Press, 2001): www.warandgender.com/wgwomwwi.htm.

site the Woolworth Building, then the tallest skyscraper in N. Y. The river here is almost exactly a mile wide, but at first glance it seemed little more than a stone's throw away.

Once the 337th had gotten all its personnel and accoutrements aboard, the ferryboat lost no time in getting underway. It headed downstream in the direction of the upper bay and presently we caught a glimpse way off on Bedloes Island of the colossal figure of Liberty holding aloft her torch, and beyond the water glittering in the brilliant sunshine. We rounded Battery Park at the tip of Manhattan and headed up the East River.[13] A mile farther on we passed under the famous Brooklyn Bridge and a bit beyond that the Manhattan Bridge. We passed the Brooklyn Navy Yard on the right, then rounded a curve in the river and headed north. We passed under the Williamsburg Bridge and continued on some two miles until we reached the Long Island R. R. terminal just beyond Newtown Creek. About a mile beyond we could see the Queensboro Bridge crossing the east and west channels separated by Welfare Island.

The 377th clambered into the Long Island Railroad Station, a bustling, crowded, clamorous place, dark and gloomy, and scrambled aboard a waiting string of cars, which soon began moving, gratefully, without the usual interminable delay which we were accustomed to take for granted. We proceeded at a moderate pace through the congestion of metropolitan Brooklyn, which in due time began to thin out somewhat. Our journey did not take over half an hour or a distance of some sixteen miles, I believe. At this point we detrained, as it were, at the edge of an extensive camp, which we learned was called Camp Mills.[14] I was never able to pinpoint its exact location on the map. It

13. Battery Park is a 25-acre public park facing New York Harbor at the southern tip of Manhattan. It takes its name from the artillery batteries stationed there by the Dutch and British.

14. Named in honor of Maj. Gen. Albert L. Mills, who received the Congressional Medal of Honor for gallantry at Santiago, Cuba, July 1, 1898, Camp Mills began life as a temporary tent camp in September 1917. Located in Nassau County, Long Island, New York, about ten miles from the eastern boundary of New York City, it continued to serve as an embarkation camp, with wooden barracks as well as tents, until it was abandoned in March 1920 (http://freepages.military.rootsweb.ancestry.com/\cacunithistories/camp_mills.htm).

was not a camp of barracks, but of tents, with enough cots in each to accommodate some four or six men. It was in the vicinity of Hempstead, which we sometimes visited during our week or so stay there. We noticed that the cab drivers parked here kept soliciting fares to "Rockaway Beach," which apparently was the nearest such resort [to] that area, located straight south on Long Island Sound.

One characteristic of Camp Mills was that airplanes were flying overhead off and on all day long, there apparently being an airport in the vicinity. I assume it might have been one or both of two airports on the coast off to the southwest, now known as John F. Kennedy Airport or Floyd Bennett Field. We did not do any drilling during our short stay here, except for the usual setting up exercises and the morning roll calls. The weather was unseasonably hot and a great number of ice cream bricks were consumed during that period, there being a well patronized commissary a couple of blocks away. That sultry week however was one of relaxation, and loafing, wandering about the camp or taking in shows in Hempstead.

That is, until the twenty-second. We were aroused early that morning, before dawn. We got our chow and coffee outdoors and down the line somewhere in the semi-dark. All over the camp, as far as the eye could reach, bon-fires were throwing an eerie light among flickering shadows. All around was the blaring of bugles and sounds of commotion, the tramping of feet, not only on all sides but from the farther distances. Off to one side we could barely discern a company of infantry marching past in their new wrapped leggings and oversea caps, with rifles shouldered and the newly issued "tin hats" slung over their packs. The 85th, it seemed, was moving out. Our turn did not come until later. In the meantime a rosy glow began to suffuse the sky in the east and presently the sun began to peep over the horizon. Finally there came that familiar raucous bellow and in short course our company was headed back to the railroad tracks where a line of coaches was waiting. We clambered aboard, wondering where we were headed now. The first destination, we soon found out, was the same Long Island Railroad station where we had entrained a week before, and on the pier just outside was waiting a similar ferryboat, on which we embarked as before. We now reversed our course, heading down the East River gawking and marveling at the lofty, close-packed wall of stupendous buildings on our right as we again passed under the three lower bridges, and skirted Battery Park. The sun burned down, and it was unbearably hot. We moved up the Hudson for some distance, it seemed, but eventually pulled up alongside a long warehouse, that was more like a covered pier extending out over the river.

We filed off the gangplank of the ferryboat and then assembled inside this spacious, gloomy barn structure. We were here served refreshments by a group of friendly ladies associated with some organization. In due course of time we proceeded single file up the gangplank to board what seemed to us a huge transport moored alongside the pier. Our company, along with several others was assigned to the forward deck and compartment below. The deck was cluttered with all manner of hoisting machinery and blocks and derricks, lifeboats swung along the side covered with tarpaulin, ventilators, hatches, a latrine, a lofty pile of rafts, etc., etc. There was the huge superstructure in the center of the ship, where the officers and some nurses headed for overseas service were quartered, also the ship's officers and crew members, the galleys, the huge smokestacks looming above, the cabins, parlors and promenade decks (which we were never to see) or the massive engines and coal bins down below. The ship's outer hull was camouflaged with bizarre streakings of zig-zag lines and configurations in various colors. Our ship, we saw, was yclept [named] the *Anchises*. (Anchises, we remembered, was the aged father of Aeneas, whom the latter carried out of burning Troy on his back.)

Once established on board, we were issued a canvas hammock and a place designated to hang it down below decks, also a life jacket which we were strictly ordered to wear at all times night and day, and a card designating the pile of life [rafts] where each was to assemble in case of emergency. Also we were shown the mess tables, running in a series up against the ship's side at right angles and below the portholes running the length of the ship.

Once established, each left his packs beneath where his hammock was fastened, and the area below being hot, stuffy and pervaded with a disagreeable odor, most of us went up on deck to gaze at the intriguing surroundings, despite the ferocity of the after noonday heat.

We watched a derrick swing a net full of barracks bags aboard the

Anchises. In so doing two or three of them rolled loose and fell into the river, sinking immediately. I fervently hoped it wasn't mine.

Somewhat later in the afternoon, about four o'clock or thereabouts, a couple of tug boats made contact with the *Anchises* and began to maneuver it out into midstream, after which we began to move slowly down toward the lower bay. The Boelens boys and I were perched high on the edge of a pile of rafts, feet hanging over the Hudson some 30 feet below on the starboard side. The view was superb, breathtaking. The continuous row of piers on both sides and the tall skyscrapers slid slowly by. It was a Sunday afternoon, and among the other shipping, there was a number of pleasure boats with the vertical Corliss engines pumping away headed upstream.[15] The decks were crowded with gay crowds in holiday attire, and they all waved and fluttered handkerchiefs as we passed them and we likewise returned their greetings as enthusiastically. The sight must have been something to stir their imagination, too — the grotesquely striped and streaked transport and the solid mass of olive drab figures lining the decks and railings above, all off to dubious, hazardous adventure and an uncertain future.

15. Corliss steam engines, invented in 1859 by the American engineer George Henry Corliss, offered the best thermal efficiency of any type of nineteenth-century steam engine. Although typically used as stationary engines to provide power to factories and mills, small versions of the engine were used on steam launches such as those Anderson saw in the Hudson River.

CHAPTER TWO

Passage from New York to England

When President Woodrow Wilson concluded that he could no longer keep the United States out of World War I, he proceeded with war plans despite the fact that his army was in no way prepared to fight, or, for that matter, even prepared to transport its troops to Europe. While European armies had been suffering casualties in the millions, the United States Army remained stagnant: it consisted of about 125,000 men under arms and an additional 80,000 reservists in various stages of preparedness. Most lacked basic weapons, uniforms, and equipment for modern warfare. Although Wilson did send one division shortly after the declaration of war, as a show of good faith, the U.S. military force was totally unprepared to assume a meaningful role in the conflict. It took nearly a year to get draftees such as Godfrey Anderson ready for service and get them transported to Europe. Even then, most of them were sent into action with only a few weeks of training; they needed additional training in Europe before they would be ready for front-line duty. The logistics of drafting, clothing, arming, feeding, training, and transporting nearly two million new soldiers was a huge undertaking. The army needed new training facilities, supply sources, embarkation camps, and land and sea transportation. Initially, there were no camps located near the docks, so troops marched directly from arriving trains to transport ships.[1]

1. Mark Henry and Stephen Walsh, *The U.S. Army of World War I* (Oxford: Os-

Most of the responsibility for outfitting training camps and moving troops fell to the U.S. Quartermaster General's office. Transporting them to Europe fell to the Quartermaster General's Water Transport Branch, which, before the declaration of war, had begun a survey and examination of every vessel under the American flag that could be adapted for the transportation of troops and animals. The order to outfit the vessels for troop transport followed immediately after the declaration of war. Ultimately, American and British vessels, as well as seized German ships, transported nearly two million Americans to Great Britain and France. The initial convoy of ten troop ships and four animal vessels got underway in June 1917, but it was months before the system became fully operational.[2]

Initially a trickle compared to the armies already in action, the U.S. Army became a swelling stream of hundreds of thousands, until by the war's end, more than two million Americans made up nearly 25 percent of the Allied army, with still more on the way. By the time of the armistice, the United States had suffered 50,000 dead in just a few months of action, and though their casualties and deaths were miniscule by European standards, if the war had continued, the U.S. Army would have played an increasingly important — and deadly — role.

Godfrey Anderson's unpleasant Atlantic crossing, aboard the British vessel *Anchises,* with unfamiliar and unappetizing food, was the first time he had ever been away from the Midwest, much less on an ocean-going vessel. It was an experience shared by many. It was a young, generally enthusiastic, but inexperienced army that was led largely by "ninety-day wonder" officers, who had been recruited from American colleges and universities and now led companies intended to be 250 strong — but often smaller — that were half country boys, few of whom had ventured far from home before. With his high school diploma and interest in history, Godfrey Anderson was something of an exception: only 21 percent of his peers had completed grammar school, and 38 percent were deemed unable to read or write.[3]

After they landed, the subsequent railroad journey through the En-

---

prey, 2003), pp. 3-12; Henry G. Sharpe, *The Quartermaster Corps in the Year 1917 in the World War* (New York: Century Company, 1921), p. 361.

2. Sharpe, *Quartermaster Corps,* pp. 349-59.

3. Sharpe, *Quartermaster Corps,* p. 6.

glish countryside introduced these Americans to unfamiliar scenes and ultimately sent them home with a broader perception of the world than that of any preceding generation of Americans. Private Godfrey Anderson, who loved books and history, took it all in with a sense of awe and adventure. He and his fellow hospital unit members had little appreciation for the horrors of the war taking place a few miles beyond the English Channel. And they certainly had no knowledge or understanding of President Wilson's decision that was to make their war experience different from that of nearly every other United States soldier.

"Our homeland was receding farther and farther behind us . . ."

Slowly we proceeded past the tip of Manhattan and into the Upper Bay. Far off to the left was Coney Island teeming with holiday crowds; on the right we were approaching, then presently passing Bedloes Island with the lady holding high her torch. We had reached a point about three miles down the bay when the ship slackened to a halt and the anchors dropped with a rattle and crash. Evidently we were to [remain] here for the night. The sun was off to the west and the view looking back toward New York was beautiful beyond compare. The lofty towers were suffused on the one side with a golden effulgence by the rays of the setting sun, standing out in bright contrast to the violet and purple shadows on the other, a fabulous vista as of some ethereal fairyland. We were served a skimpy mess, but most of us returned to the deck and watched the sun go down and darkness fall and after a while the stars came out and the moon began to rise. A variety of indistinct sounds floated out from the surrounding distances amid the lapping of the waves below. Along the far horizons a million lights twinkled.

The night was still hot and most of the service-men had brought up their hammocks and strung them up in every conceivable place on the deck. I managed to find a place just over some hoisting machinery, not the best place to land if one should fall over the side. I could not see too much of what arrangements the others had made, it being too dark and I speedily fell into a profound slumber and did not awaken until a new day had dawned next morning.

I now could look around me with more visibility. Hammocks were strung up in every conceivable place on that foredeck. One was hanging precariously over the extreme bow; another was suspended high up alongside the davits in such a manner that had the occupant inadvertently toppled out of the hammock he would have taken a nose dive into the Upper Bay.[4] The weather continued lovely but warm as it had been for quite a spell now. We lounged about all morning, reveling in the thrilling and exciting vistas in all directions. It was about noon or shortly after that the grating of the anchor chains alerted us to the fact that the ship was about to get underway. Imperceptibly it moved slowly downstream toward the narrows between lower Brooklyn and Staten Island, with Fort Hamilton on the one side and Fort Wadsworth on the other.[5] Gradually it emerged into the open waters of the Lower Bay. Somewhere in here we passed the anchored Ambrose Light Ship where the pilots who guide the ships entering or leaving through the complicated traffic of N. Y. harbor embark or disembark.

Slowly the shoreline began to recede in the distance. One thing aroused my curiosity and wonder: I noticed thousands of loaves of bread floating in the water all around. I had brought along a book to read, Stevenson's "Kidnapped," and I thought to pass the time looking into it now. However I could not get interested in it, there was too much excitement all around, I guess, and I never did finish it. Besides I

4. A davit is a mechanical arm with a winch used to lower life rafts and raise spare parts onto a vessel.

5. Fort Hamilton, established in the southwestern corner of Brooklyn during the American Revolution, is today one of several posts in the Military District of Washington, supporting the Army National Guard and the United States Army Reserve (http://www.harbordefensemuseum.com/). Likewise, Fort Wadsworth defended New York Harbor for nearly 200 years before the last military tenant, the Navy, departed in 1995, officially turning it over to the Department of the Interior. In 1997, Fort Wadsworth opened to the public as part of Gateway National Recreation Area (http://www.statenislandusa.com/pages/ft_wadsworth.html).

was bothered with an unusual headache and dizziness, which I later realized was a symptom of seasickness, but which disappeared later in the afternoon. In fact this slight suggestion of seasickness was all I ever experienced in my subsequent and often stormy seafaring ventures.

But one thing became presently apparent. We soon discovered we were in a convoy of 15 transports, all as bizarrely camouflaged as our own ship. They were spread out in a formation occupying perhaps a square mile (it is difficult to judge distances on open water) but as each became more or less familiar to us as time went on we noticed that they never changed their relative positions in the convoy. As time went on we noticed that two destroyers kept pace with us, but far to the south and barely distinguishable along the horizon. We spent that second night about the same as the night before. The life preservers made a good substitute for a pillow. However, we noticed none had their hammocks slung in the precarious positions mentioned before, nor indeed were there as many sleeping on the outer deck as before.

Another day dawned. The routine remained monotonously the same, as day followed day. The route of the convoy was a swing to the northeast paralleling Nova Scotia and Newfoundland. The weather grew considerably cooler, and sleeping on deck was abandoned for the regular places apportioned for hammocks below. The odor below however was disgustingly nauseous. Most of the other times were spent on the open deck in the brisk and invigorating winds. One annoying thing we found out: the salt water from the faucets would not lather up the shaving soap. There was something depressing along about eventide when the sun was sinking behind the watery horizon, and darkness began to fall, and as we watched the last glow in the west, and realizing that our homeland was receding farther and farther behind us every day.

The *Anchises* was a British owned ship and the food served in the mess halls was simply execrable.[6] I don't remember just what was served, but I soon lost interest in the so-called food and seldom showed up for

6. The vessel Anderson sailed on was the first of three British vessels named *Anchises*. Built in 1911, this first *Anchises* was the property of the Ocean Steamship Co., Ltd. From 1914 to October 1917, she served as an HMATT (Her Majesty's Auxiliary Troop Transport) for Australian troops. Thereafter, she began transporting U.S. troops to Europe. The *Anchises* weighed 10,046 tons and was capable of speeds up to 10 knots. (*The Ships List:* www.theshipslist.com/ships/lines/index.htm.)

Their basic training over, Pvt. Godfrey Anderson and the other members of the 337th Field Hospital Unit traveled by railroad to New York, where they boarded HMATT *Anchises*, which was bound for England. (State Library of Victoria, Melbourne, Australia, H91.325179I)

mess. Instead of coffee, chicory was served, and there was always on hand a certain greenish jam, which tasted as though concocted from limes, the standard British remedy for scurvy. I remember once when faint from hunger, I ventured down to attempt to appease the gnawing pangs. The first course was a pan of tripe, which is the bag of a cow cut into squares immersed in a repelling white sauce. It had the consistency of rubber and [was] impossible to chew. After that a dish of fried fish came down the table. The whole mess was spoiled and stank to high heaven. It went down the table untouched and out the porthole. Nauseated by the unsavory concoctions and the sickening stench that permeated the decks below, I beat it for the open airs above and went on a prolonged fast. We had left the states so precipitately that I had no cash on hand, so could purchase nothing at the ship's commissary which opened for a couple of hours during the day. Luckily I discovered where the potatoes were stored so I subsisted for the final days aboard ship on raw potatoes.

And so one monotonous day succeeded another. There was no drilling nor setting up exercises, except for an occasional life raft drill to expedite efficiency in reaching the proper stations in case of emergency. The same unvarying positions of the sister transports continued unchanged. The two destroyers kept the same pace in the barely visible far distance. There were no lights showing anywhere at night. Once or twice there were dense fogs and visibility was practically non-existent. Our ship, and I presume the others, towed a barrel by rope at the rear, which threw up a white spray visible to the lookout on the ship behind.

The weather was often chilly in those northern latitudes beyond the Gulf Stream. Sometimes there were winds and high waves. On one occasion there was a violent storm, the waves loomed on either side like rolling mountains and the ship pitched and rolled in an alarming fashion. Many of the men became seasick. There was a latrine up front with a standing trough along the wall for urinating. The first impulse of a seasick soldier was to rush in and throw up in this trough. The drainage end had become clogged with the residue of their last meal. When the ship rolled the mixture of urine and vomit would violently be diverted to the end of the trough and it would bang up against the wall with a tremendous splash to flood the floor with the disgusting mess. A guard was set at the door to prevent puking in the trough. The victim would rush in with but one objective in mind, paid no heed to the peremptory order, would heave up his guts, as it were, into the trough, then turn his sickly green visage to the guard in blank incomprehension. I noticed one group huddled miserably by the rail on the windward side. One of them gave a sudden heave, directed overboard. However, the wind caught up the glutinous mess, and spread it like an enveloping veil over the entire group.

On the Sunday a week after we had left Manhattan the weather turned lovely, and an impromptu entertainment was arranged on deck. The officers and lady nurses appeared on the upper decks amidships all in good humor. There were boxing matches and a variety of songs. The one I remember went like this: "The Kaiser sent a million men away to fight, so he could have a different sweetheart every night. (Chorus) O if you're crazy about the women you're not crazy at all."

We were now gradually approaching the end of our journey, which however was in the danger zone. The weather had moderated, there were occasional rain squalls, but the days were mostly pleasant and sunny. We had re-entered the bland waters of the Gulf Stream evidently. It was around ten o'clock of such a morning that there was suddenly something of a commotion off in the direction of the destroyers, off in the distance. We were hurriedly ordered below where we milled about adjusting our life jackets and wondering what was going on. It seems that submarines had put in an appearance. Before going below we caught a glimpse of those two destroyers cavorting about like a couple of terriers pursuing a rat. There were sounds of distant gunfire. Presently all was quiet again and we returned back to the foredeck. The transports were all intact, and the destroyers were back in position on the horizon. What had happened we never found out. Rumors had it that two subs had appeared and that one had been destroyed. (By the way, subsequent rumors had it that the *Anchises* was sent to the bottom on her return trip.)[7]

The night following proved to be our last aboard ship and the following day found us somewhere in the Irish Sea. In the distance barely visible loomed a hazy promontory — the Isle of Man some one said. Later in the day a distant coastline appeared, and in due time we found we were entering the estuary of the river Mersey. Some three miles further upstream we were warped up at a temporary mooring, amid a forest of shipping, various piers and warehouses. We had reached Liverpool at last! It had begun to rain — a heavy downpour — and we stood about in whatever shelter was at hand staring at whatever could be seen from our cramped in and limited point of view. Liverpool, the second largest city in Britain, had at that time a population of nearly 850,000. It is the principal seaport of England. It is located on the right (east) bank of the estuary of the Mersey about three miles from the open sea. Opposite Liverpool the river is about a mile [wide], but above the city it expands and forms a basin three miles across. The most remarkable sites of Liverpool are the docks which flank the Mersey for some six or seven miles.

After a seemingly interminable cooling of our heels the ship was maneuvered and warped to a different pier. The rain had stopped and a late afternoon sun was trying to break through in the west. We were suddenly ordered to begin moving various equipment, boxes and baggage from the transport to a string of railroad cars. The life jackets which we had worn continuously for nearly two weeks, thirteen days to be exact, were finally turned in along with our hammocks on a sidetrack a short distance away. To reach this we had to pass through a warehouse with open ends facing the pier. Along one side was stored a great pile of gunny sacks containing brown sugar. Half starved as I was, I lost no time in digging out greedy handfuls of sugar each time I passed through. Alongside the railroad track were parked some of those diminutive boxcars that are standard in Great Britain. A group of Yanks, finding something ludicrous in these tiny (by Western stan-

7. This rumor was untrue. The *Anchises* survived World War I, but not World War II. German bombers sank her off Mersey in 1941, with a loss of twelve lives (*Order of Battle:* www.unsw.adfa.edu.au/~rmallett/).

dards) boxcars, were having a gay old time, laughing and whooping, as they easily pushed one back and forth on the rails.

Here we had a better view of our surroundings. There was an impressive looking building off at one side, surrounded by a high brick wall. Instead of barbed wire atop this wall, pieces of broken glass had been set in the concrete coping. A further inspection of adjoining walls around other buildings demonstrated that this was the standard method of keeping out intruders, at least in this area. When finally everything had been transferred, the 337th was ordered to pick up all their packs and equipment and line up for a roll call and check up. Then they were marched off to the waiting train and were allotted seats on board. Those British coaches were different and strange to us. Instead of an aisle down the center of the coaches, as we were used to, each coach was divided into compartments each with two seats the width of the coach and facing each other. However, the road beds, as we had reason to confirm later, are beautifully kept up and the railroad service was fast and efficient

Anyway we finally got away shortly after dusk on what was called the Midland Railroad. . . . There were no latrines available on the coaches, as we are accustomed to in the States and the call of nature could not be deferred. The only available way for relief was through the windows. One had to be a bit circumspect because for a while a continuous stream sailed past alongside the coaches and the suction through an open window could shower one with an odoriferous spray. Suddenly without warning the train would pass through one of those small village stations that lined the way at unpredictable intervals and the people on the platforms must have been amazed and mystified and perhaps sprinkled a bit as the train passed through.

Brookwood Station proved to be the end of the line for us. Here we disembarked, as it were, and lined up somewhere beside the tracks and then headed off in a southwesterly direction for about a mile or so. Here we entered what was called Stoney Castle Camp, an extensive area covered with hundreds of tents, which apparently were to be the temporary rendezvous of the 85th Division.[8] Our company was assigned a section

8. Stoney Castle Camp, near Brookwood Railway Station, about thirty miles southwest of London, was a major embarkation and receiving camp during World War I. It was located on open land adjacent to Brookwood Cemetery, also known as

near the south end of the camp alongside which extended a sort of woodland or copse. There were no cots supplied and we spread our blankets on the bare ground and established ourselves as best we could, each tent accommodating some four persons. It was approaching mid morning and we were directed to a place down the line where chow was dished out. As my stomach felt as if it were touching my backbone, due to the niggardly and unsavory rations served aboard the *Anchises* for two weeks, I lost no time in hitting the chow line. The food was served from tables out of doors and you ate sitting on the ground. The main dish was a mutton stew — nothing ever tasted so good. The cooks and rations were all good old U.S.A. and you were served all you wanted, without quibble. I downed three mess kits of mutton stew with great relish, but have never been able to stand mutton stew since.

The method of washing mess kits after these outdoor mess servings left much to be desired. There were two dixies of hot water set to one side; in one you gave the mess kit a preliminary swishing and then gave it a final rinsing in the other. In no time at all the contents of the first dixie was more like a vegetable soup while the other was more like contaminated bouillon.[9] The mess kit was usually coated with a thin layer of grease at all times.

The Boelens brothers and I wandered about most of the afternoon; we visited a pub at Brookwood and each bought a lemon drink in a glass bottle at 10 pence. (The favorite drink of the average Briton seemed to be brews called stout and ale.) We paid a dime for each which the proprietors, a man and a woman, accepted dubiously but good naturedly. Those glass bottles were a curiosity to us. They were not capped with metal and crimped as we are used to, but consisted of a little glass ball set in a hollow in the neck of the bottle and were punched out somehow. Around sunset a band way off played the Star Spangled Banner

---

the London Necropolis, established in 1852 to house the city's dead. A military cemetery established at the site in 1917 for British war dead has a four-acre section containing the graves of 468 Americans and a memorial commemorating 563 others with no known grave. Nearby is the Brookwood Russia Memorial erected in 1983 to commemorate forces of the British Commonwealth who died in Russia in World War I and World War II.

9. "Dixies" are large, two-compartment metal sinks for use in places that serve food and wash dishes on a large scale.

while the Stars & Stripes, floating on a high flagstaff in the distance, was lowered, while companies all over the camp as far as the eye could reach were standing at attention. Later in the evening well after roll call the two Boelens boys and myself stepped out of camp through the woodland mentioned and took a hike cross country toward Aldershot some three or four miles away. Aldershot, a town of more than 25,000 inhabitants, is a great military center with an extensive military hospital. Extensive military [operations] are held here from time to time. It is said that Julius Caesar had a camp here in the Roman period. Night had fallen when we approached the town. We did not go there but viewed it from a hillside to the east. As we watched, a hospital train with wounded soldiers from the front in France pulled into the station. The thought struck us that we had better get back into camp before we got an AWOL. We hurried back in the darkness and managed to avoid the guards and sneak back into camp.

There was no drilling during our stay here, but nearly every day the company went on a hike around the area surrounding the camp. The country roads wind around among copses and woodlands, a beautiful countryside it is and the weather during the time was sunny and pleasant. We would be marching along one of those winding tree lined roads singing one of those ribald obscene songs such as soldiers have sung from time immemorial, when, rounding a turn, we would unexpectedly run into some small hamlet. Immediately the officer shouted "attention," and we marched thru the village in silence, only to resume the bawdy songs when we had passed through it. On our usual hikes we passed a handsome red brick residence just outside the camp. This was once the home of the African explorer Henry M. Stanley and his grave was near the roadside where we passed. There was a tall natural stone over the grave on which was carved the name by which he was known to the African natives but which I do not recall.[10] Hanging over the grave was a strange looking tree transplanted from Africa, a monkey-tail tree I believe it was called.[11]

10. Stanley's stone bears the name Bula Matari ("breaker of rocks"), his name among Africans in the Belgian Congo, as it was known then.

11. The monkey tree is an Andean evergreen species that can grow to be 50-75 feet tall and resembles a tangled mass of monkey's tails.

That was the routine of that first week — the bugles at reveille, the roll calls, the cross country hikes, the in-between loafing, the interminable rattling and screaming of the Southwestern Railroad in the distance, the short arm[s] inspections, the bands at sunset, and lastly the bugles blowing the final mournful taps.[12] Then the aches and sore hips from sleeping on the hard ground. Some of the men went into the thickets close by and brought back armfuls of hay to upholster their sleeping pallets a bit.

Sometime during our second week in camp a group from our company was selected to go to Aldershot to get a bit of practical experience among wounded soldiers.[13] We got aboard our army truck which hauled us over to a handsome brick barracks in that town where we set up our quarters in a good sized room. Afterwards some of us wandered about the town; it was largely in a military setting with many barracks and parade grounds. In the evenings especially the streets were crowded with pedestrians, limey soldiers and pretty girls available to be escorted around town. There was a bandstand in the center of town and a classy band was playing, largely military marches. The next day we were each assigned to a different ward to make ourselves useful, or as it seemed mostly to absorb atmosphere.

The nurses didn't have much respect for us so-called medics, being as we were mostly unsophisticated ignoramuses. One night, however, we became useful. About midnight we were aroused and ordered down to the depot. A troop train with casualties from the front was coming in alongside the military hospital building and we were detailed to meet it. The coaches were fitted up with bunks along each side, on which were placed the wounded Limeys on stretchers. Our job was to carry the stretchers from the train to the hospital wards. I have no idea how many there were but it took us quite a while to empty the coaches. We noticed one thing: all the local Limey orderlies who were supposed

---

12. "Short arms inspections" was the soldiers' slang term for medical inspections intended to identify signs of sexually transmitted diseases.

13. The British Army established a permanent camp near Aldershot in 1854. Aldershot Military Hospital was opened at the camp soon after its founding to provide care for British military personnel. Prior to World War I, it was renamed Cambridge Hospital, and it was the first base hospital to receive casualties directly from the western front.

to help us had disappeared and left all the toting to us. The next day when we went back to the wards, which were now well filled, we got a preview of all manner of wounds, gunshot, shrapnel, mustard gas and various amputations. Later in the day we went in to watch the technique used with leg amputations. There was a poor fellow with a leg amputated just above the knee. The idea was to glue four canvas strips to the leg, which already were attached to a rope going over a pulley and to attach [it] to a weight. The idea was to stretch the skin to properly cover the stump. The lady nurse apparently didn't like Yankees and made small effort to conceal it. She had a pot of hot glue and explained that the procedure was to try it on someone's arm to see if the temperature was not too hot for the patient. Without giving me a chance to get set she took me unaware and slapped a brushful of hot glue on my arm. It was excruciatingly hot but rather than give her any satisfaction I made no sign of any discomfort. She asked if it was too hot, and without thinking, I nonchalantly said, "No." Judging by my expression that such was the case she immediately slapped a brushful of that hot glue on the patient's tender skin just above the amputation. The poor fellow let out a terrible shriek and I realized I had made a mistake, as well as had the nurse.

Another mix-up I got into here was this. The surgeon had a circumcision case and showed me how it was to be dressed. I didn't understand that I was supposed to dress it from then on. When the surgeon came back some days later and saw no renewed bandage, he reproached me in no uncertain terms.

We were in Aldershot about a week. During that week we lived on practically a starvation basis. It was like the *Anchises* all over again, except that the food was clean. About all we got each meal was a thin sandwich, more of that ubiquitous green jam and a bowl of tea. We certainly were glad to get back to Stoney Castle Camp and that good old USA grub.

In the meantime we found that in contrast to our week of fasting in Aldershot, our comrades who had remained behind had been given a pass to London, to our great envy. However, we had scarcely got back when the rumor went around that the 337th was headed for Russia. It was not official, apparently, but along about morning of the twenty-sixth we were ordered to break camp, shoulder our packs and march in fours back to Brookwood Station. Sure enough, there was a train standing there on a sidetrack and we were ordered aboard. After some delay in getting each compartment properly apportioned the train began to move and we realized we were leaving Brookwood, no doubt forever.

The American North Russia Expeditionary force, as we learned later, consisted of the 339th infantry, one battalion of the 310 Engineers, the 337th Ambulance Co., and the 337th Field Hospital. It was through some mix-up that the 337th companies were selected instead of the 339th Ambulance and Field Hospital Companies.

CHAPTER THREE

Newcastle to Archangel

Godfrey Anderson had been a soldier for only three months when he learned of the Allied decision that was to alter the direction of his military experience. Instead of caring for sick and wounded soldiers in Allied hospitals in England or France, he was to spend the remainder of his military career in northern Russia.

He knew where he was headed, though he did not understand exactly why. Even without the uncertainty of what might be awaiting him at the end of the voyage, he had reason to be anxious about this trip through the North Sea to Murmansk — and then on to Archangel. The North Sea was full of German submarines, and seldom did Allied vessels travel the region unless they were part of an escorted convoy. However, Allied leaders were in such a hurry to get troops to Russia that they sent four unescorted vessels to Murmansk, which is on the Kola Peninsula very near the northern tips of both Finland and Norway. To avoid giving U-boats easy targets, the transports traveled erratic, zigzag paths and kept lookouts on constant alert.

Yet, as it turned out, submarines were not the greatest threat facing the convoy. The British troop ships *Somali, Tydens, Nagoya,* and *Czar* had scarcely cleared the Newcastle harbor when physicians on board noticed a disturbing development. An unusually high number of the troops had fallen ill, and though the soldiers may have thought so, the culprit was not the British food. The highly contagious influenza, the Spanish flu that had broken out in Spain in May 1918 and quickly spread throughout Europe, had become especially virulent among the troops in the trenches of the Great War, and it had found its way aboard ship. For those headed to Russia on the troop transports, there was little the physicians and medical assistants of the 337th could do to stem the flu's spread. Just as it is today, the standard treatment called for bed rest, a lot of fluids, and antibiotics for any ancillary infection. Unfortunately, antibiotics and other medications that would have been useful had remained behind in Newcastle when the ships departed, and there was little to be done except make the sufferers as comfortable as possible.

The youth and general good health of the soldiers would have seemed to help them battle the disease. In fact, however, the pattern of the flu was counterintuitive: the disease assumed its most virulent form among the youngest and healthiest. Later research has concluded that the virus caused an overreaction of the body's immune system; thus, the stronger the immune system, the stronger the reaction. The virus ravaged young adults, while the weaker immune systems of children and middle-aged adults produced weaker cases of flu, causing fewer deaths. With few medicines and a limited understanding of the disease, Anderson's 337th Hospital Unit's first significant duty found them putting their own health at risk while attempting to provide care for Spanish flu victims.

After a brief stop at the port of Murmansk — just long enough for the flu virus to go ashore — the troop transports moved on to Archangel, a remote frontier city on Dvina Bay of the White Sea.[1] Once again, the still-

---

1. Modern Archangel dates from the construction of a trading outpost and fort in 1553. A great bazaar and trading hall, built between 1668 and 1684, furthered trade activity. Prior to the founding of St. Petersburg in 1703, Archangel was Russia's principal seaport. It was open to all nations and busy during the six months it was ice-free (May-October). At the time that Allied troops arrived in 1918, Archangel was a shipping and industrial city whose factories produced linen, leather, canvas, cordage, mats, tallow, potash, and beer. Each year timber, flax, linseed, oats, flour, pitch, tar, hide, and reed mat exports valued at 12 million pounds sterling shipped from its docks. Imports were much smaller, with most sent to the Russian interior by river, canal, and railway line. The Archangel harbor, dug out to 184 feet around the docks, was accessible to any ocean-going vessels. As the sparsely populated region's religious and cultural center, it was the seat of a bishop and, in addition to the cathedral, featured a monastery and seminary, as well as a museum, school of navigation, and naval hospital. *Classic Encyclopedia*, based on *Encyclopedia Britannica*, 11th ed., 1911 (http://www.1911encyclopedia.org/Archangel,_Russia).

active flu virus came ashore with the troops and spread to the local population. The city had limited resources to either deal with the flu or accommodate the Allied expeditionary force, and chaos was reigning in Archangel even before the troops arrived. The British had forced a change from a
pro-Bolshevik local government to one more amenable to Allied wishes;
however, it was weak, ineffective, and corrupt. The expeditionary forces
appropriated public and private buildings and turned them into the hospitals, warehouses, barracks, headquarters offices, and support facilities
that they needed. In a couple of months the worst of the flu had subsided,
the buildings were outfitted, and the troops had become reasonably comfortable. Unfortunately, they did not have much time to enjoy their surroundings before their orders moved them out into the region's small villages and surrounding swamps and forests.

"No land in sight and the outlook was bleak . . ."

We pulled into the station at Newcastle on Tyne in the late afternoon and
we piled out and lined up in columns of fours. Noted for its shipbuilding
yards and manufacture of locomotives and its iron industry, Newcastle
was also known for its extensive mines and coal shipping. It was an
ancient-looking place, sooty and begrimed. The streets were cramped and
winding and paved with cobblestones, and so narrow that when we clat-
tered over the treacherous footing the outside man had to walk on the
sidewalk, jostling the bystanders who stood gawking at us and wondering
who we were and what we were doing up in this area. The street led down
a very steep hill and the road was so ill paved that we could barely keep our
footing, but after we stumbled along for a while we came finally to a dock
on the river, where several camouflaged transports were moored alongside. We went single file up the gangplank of one of these, the *Somali* it
was named, and somehow got ourselves established aboard.[2] The latter

2. Launched in 1901 by the Peninsular and Oriental Steam Navigation Company,

part of the day had been overcast and evening descended rather early, it seemed. The hold was quite crowded, and it was up to us to find a spot on which to bed down during the night. My buddy (one Gerrit Boelens from Spring Lake, Mich.) and I slept right in the center of the floor, right over a slat that didn't bother us too much. His brother Herman had become ill in England and had been left behind in the hospital at Aldershot. Later he died there.

Sometime after midnight, when spying eyes were less likely to note our departure, we began floating down the Tyne in complete silence and obscurity to the North Sea, some nine miles distant. Despite the bustle and congestion we managed to get a fairly good night's sleep. The grub aboard the *Somali* was somewhat better than that of the *Anchises,* when crossing the Atlantic. Later we went out on deck to look around. It was a dark day, lowering and gloomy, with a leaden, choppy sea. There was no land in sight and the outlook was bleak. We noticed we were in a convoy of four British troop ships all similarly streaked and striped to camouflage them. We also noticed that although we were in a dangerous submarine zone, there were no destroyers to escort us through the danger zone. We later learned that the other ships were the *Tydens,* the *Nagoya* and the *Czar,* the latter carrying Italian troops and headed for Murmansk. We also noticed that there was a swivel gun mounted on the foredeck with a British marine in attendance constantly. Every one of us was encumbered with a lifejacket to be worn night and day. The ship kept zig-zagging constantly, always on the lookout for submarines.[3]

---

the passenger and cargo vessel *Somali* was 450 feet long with a breadth of 52 feet; she was scrapped in Copenhagen in 1923 (www.clydebuiltships.co.uk).

3. Submarines were a very real threat to the troop ships. World War I was the first war to feature submarine warfare, and the navies of Great Britain, Germany, Russia, Japan, the Netherlands, and the United States all possessed underwater vessels capable of sinking military and merchant ships. Germany had by far the largest submarine fleet, beginning the war with more than twenty boats, and building another 345 during its duration. Initially, while they could sink military vessels on sight, German submariners observed prize regulations for merchant ships, requiring them to surface, stop the ships, and safely evacuate their occupants before sinking the vessels. However, this placed them at risk from defensively armed ships, so in January 1917, Germany announced that its U-boats would engage in unrestricted submarine warfare, sinking vessels carrying goods destined for Great Britain or France without warning. After Ger-

And so one day followed another with monotonous regularity. All during this part of the voyage we kept well out of sight of the Norwegian coastline, keeping between the Shetland Islands and the bulge of Norway, a distance of some 300 miles, after which we entered the Norwegian Sea. A few days later, rounding the North Cape, we entered the Barents Sea [part of the Arctic Ocean] and were now well beyond the Arctic Circle. The weather had turned unpleasantly cold and as we turned to enter the White Sea we could see snow on some point or island far to the northeast. The sudden change from the hot weather in England to the raw temperature and chilly winds of the Arctic climate was too drastic for many of the soldiers and quite a few became sick. Our overcoats had been packed in barracks bags and stored deep down in the hold so we could not put on the warmer clothing so badly needed.

What developed was the Spanish influenza, which broke out on all the ships.[4] To make matters worse, the medical supplies had somehow not gotten aboard, except for a small supply that had been brought from Camp Custer. All bunks were occupied by soldiers desperately ill, with raging fevers; others lay on stretchers, the breathing of all a rasping wheeze. The available medicine was soon exhausted. The first death occurred on the White Sea and the body was dumped to a watery grave from a tilted board. Some of our outfit suffered from sea sickness most of the way. Our long-eared friend, George Whitmore, somewhat mentally retarded, it would seem, declared emphatically that

<hr />

man submarines sank several American merchant vessels, the United States declared war in April 1917. During the course of the war, German submarines sank an estimated 5,000 Allied ships, with a loss of approximately 15,000 lives. Germany itself lost 178 submarines and over 5,000 crewmen. Douglas Botting, *The U-boats* (Alexandria, VA: Time-Life Books, 1979).

4. The 1918 Spanish flu pandemic was the result of an unusually severe and deadly virus that spread to nearly every part of the world. It lasted from March 1918 to June 1920 and may have killed as many as fifty million people worldwide. First observed among soldiers at Fort Riley, Kansas, and in Queens, New York, the disease became known as Spanish flu because it received greater press attention after it moved to Spain in November 1918. Spain was not involved in the war and had not imposed wartime censorship on its newspapers; as a result, the Spanish were the first to attribute widespread deaths to the flu. John M. Barry, *The Great Influenza: The Epic Story of the Greatest Plague in History* (New York: Viking Penguin, 2004).

this was his last boat trip and when the war was over he was going home by train by way of Chicago.

It was about our ninth or tenth day out of Newcastle that we were able to discern far on the horizon ahead what later proved to be an island. We were approaching what is known as the Dvina Delta.[5] This extensive delta is some 24 miles across and extends some 20 miles out from Archangel. This alluvial deposit had been cut up into half a dozen large islands and some half dozen smaller ones through which several channels have gouged their way. As we approached this intricate maze of islands and passages we noticed that the delta appeared to be one vast swampland covered with reeds and swamp grass of an artificial, poisonous-looking green, the whole one vast, and apparently uninhabited, godforsaken wilderness. The convoy halted at the entrance of the main channel, and a small tug came alongside the *Nagoya*, which happened to be in the lead, with a pilot to guide us through the intricate labyrinth, the other two transports following in single file. After a while the swampy patches came closer together and the channel became more like a river or canal.

Presently the swampy morass gave way to more solid ground or tundra and there were signs of some sparse habitation: here and there some wretched settlement of a few squalid shacks; an occasional stack of swamp hay piled along the shore, or some decrepit fishing schooner lying befouled and water-logged and apparently abandoned. The entire vista was dreary and desolate, the sky being heavily overcast and the vast swamps stretching interminably, unrelieved by any woodland, except for a few stunted pine trees. A few miles further on we came to what might be called the metropolis of the area — Economia or Economy Point — a sort of lumbering center, with a number of warehouses along the shore, with some barges anchored and log rafts and booms tied to the bank, a sawmill with a rusted tin roof and smoke stacks, and heaps of sawdust, board walks over the mud, and piles of rotting lumber.[6] From here on we

5. The Northern Dvina River (there is also a Western Dvina) flows north through Vologda Oblast (a Russian federal administrative district) and Arkhangelsk Oblast to the White Sea at Archangel. At a length of 465 miles, it is Russia's eleventh longest river and drains a basin of 411,000 square kilometers (http://russia.rin.ru/guides_e/4343.html).

6. Economia, or "Economy Point," was a government dockyard and merchants'

Approaching Archangel, Anderson and his fellow soldiers saw a city of about 30,000 with a low flat aspect dominated by government buildings and multispired churches. (Library of Congress, LC-DIG-ppmsc-03836)

passed a cluster of buildings here and there, too few to be called villages, all equally sordid and miserable. Whenever we passed people on shore they stared back at us, listlessly and apathetically, making no signs of greeting or friendliness, whatsoever, appearing indifferent or even hostile. At one point the channel narrowed and took a right angled turn and when the *Nagoya* took the turn and passed along between some buildings it seemed — to those on the ships behind not yet having made the turn — that she was moving up a street between the buildings.

Some time toward noon we emerged into a wide expanse of the river a couple of miles or so across, where all the transports dropped anchor. It had taken us eleven days to reach Archangel, which now lay along the left hand shore. There were a number of fishing boats anchored nearby. The people aboard ignored us completely and we got the impression that we were not welcome here.

We stood on deck and stared at the extensive vista spread out before us. The broad river extended to infinity in both directions it

---

warehouse complex about twelve miles north — and further down the Dvina River — from Archangel. *Classic Encyclopedia,* based on *Encyclopedia Britannica,* 11th ed., 1911 (http://www.1911encyclopedia.org/Archangel,_Russia).

Upon arrival, Anderson and his companions disembarked down the *Somali*'s gangway and made their way to hastily prepared quarters in Archangel. (NARS, U.S. Army Signal Corps Photograph, no. SC 39258)

seemed, and was finally lost in the far distances. The Dvina here was more like a bay or large lake. Extending from a point or peninsula at the north for a couple of miles alongside the Dvina until lost in the distance lay the port of Archangel, a city with a normal population of some 40,000. There were several handsome churches in sight, especially one majestic cathedral with half a dozen bulbous spires that was the most imposing focal point in the entire panorama.[7] There were many impressive buildings extending the entire distance, mostly stuccoed, some delicately tinted. Several sea-going ships were tied up alongside, and a myriad of fishing boats were crowded along the shore.

Bakaritza

On the other side and bit closer to us was a place called Bakaritza, also with various docks to accommodate sea-going vessels and a number of unpainted warehouses, barracks and various shacks. As we stood there gazing in the gloom of a lowering sky, a heavy rain began to fall. On one of the sister ships the band came out and, standing under cover, began to play some lively music. They had run up a flag high on the mast, and in the stiff breeze it crackled and snapped almost like pistol shots, flaunting proudly and defiantly, yet lovely as a wind whipped rose. We watched it with emotion; we had never realized before how beautiful those stars and stripes were and how much that flag meant to us, here in this apparently hostile land.

7. Anderson is probably referring to Trinity Cathedral and its five onion-domed towers. In 1929, the Communists destroyed the historic church, which was constructed in 1709 (http://en.wikipedia.org/wiki/Image:Archangel_riverbank.jpg).

I do not recall just when we left the ship, whether or not it was that same day or the next; some of the troops on other transports did spend the first night aboard ship. Eventually the *Somali* was eased over to a dock at Bakaritza, and the winches and derricks began unloading the cargo, which was transported to one of the warehouses along shore, and the sick were moved to a rather primitive Russian hospital not far away. At any rate it was late in the afternoon when we finally disembarked and reassembled on the wharf and lined up ready to march. There were a number of native Russians standing around, staring phlegmatically, silent and inscrutable, the women with shawls or babushkas over their heads, the men with shirts worn over the trousers, and with buttons along the side of the front held in place by wide belts with ornate buckles. Most of them wore boots as well as luxurious hirsute appendages.

We started off to one of the barracks to which we had been assigned. The area was swampy and we proceeded in places on duckboards and floating bridges laid over the marshy terrain.[8] The entire day had been dark and gloomy and during that comparatively short march, not quite a mile, night had fallen with surprising suddenness.[9] When we entered the large, roughly built barracks building we found ourselves in almost total darkness. The large room was completely bare, the place newly built and the outside unpainted. There was a double deck platform running down the center of the room. Some of us managed to clamber aboard and spread our blankets over the hard boards, prepared to spend the night as best we could. There were no lights and as some members of another company were to be temporarily quartered here, there was a great deal of confusion and a bit of wrangling here and there in the dark. We had by this time become accustomed to sleeping in unconventional places and I, at least, passed the night in profound slumber.

The gray light of morning awakened me, and because of the urgent call of nature, I hurriedly dressed, what little dressing there was to do, and stepped outside into what appeared to be the main street, lined by

8. "Duckboards" are boardwalks laid over wet, muddy, or cold surfaces. The term came into common usage to describe boards laid at the bottom of trenches on the western front in World War I.

9. The shortest day in Archangel is dark for all but 3 hours, 12 minutes; the longest day has 21 hours, 48 minutes of daylight.

various rude domiciles. The streets were apparently deserted, except for some strange looking birds flitting about on the ground with a continuous, raucous croaking. These were about the size and general appearance of ravens, but with a slate gray plumage. They walked about, apparently unintimidated by the presence of humans. What their ornithological names are we never learned; we referred to them as those "mud colored crows."[10]

I looked about in vain for some sort of latrine or backhouse. I was surprised to discover, a bit later, that the most ornate building in the village, which stood in the center of what may be designated as the public plaza and what I first mistook for a bandstand, was in fact the communal latrine or privy. I ascended a flight of stairs to a balcony, which ran around the octagonal building, and was enclosed by a railing and entered a good sized room. Across the center ran a row of toilet seats placed back to back.

I appropriated one of the seats and was meditating on my strange surroundings when a middle aged female walked into the room. She bowed politely and bid me, "Drastitche" (the equivalent of "good morning"). I was nonplussed, to say the least, at the customs of this strange country. Then I noticed that there were no separate compartments for men and women. Just then tough old Captain [Hugh S.] Martin came in, and looking the place over, exclaimed, "I wonder if anyone has caught the crabs in this joint?"[11]

Coming back I noticed a couple of Yiddish looking buck privates who apparently were intrigued by the currency of the realm that they

10. Most likely, Anderson is referring to hooded crows *(Corvus cornix),* also known as Scotch crows, Danish crows, and, in Ireland, grey crows: an ashy grey bird with black head, throat, wings, tail and thigh feathers, as well as a black bill, eyes, and feet. The hooded crow's habitat is northern, eastern, and southeastern Europe, as well as the Middle East. Steven Madge and Hilary Burn, *Crows and Jays: A Guide to the Crows, Jays and Magpies of the World* (London: A. & C. Black, 1994).

11. Captain Martin's reference to "crabs" was soldier's slang for lice found in pubic hair, a condition medically known as *pediculosis pubis* (the official name is *Pthirus pubis*) (http://www.emedicinehealth.com/crabs/article_em.htm).

Anderson expressed himself on the subject of lice and other miniscule creatures that tormented combat soldiers in his short essay entitled "Treatise on Cooties," which was published in the *Sentinel,* a weekly newspaper published by the American troops in Archangel (it is reprinted as Appendix C at the end of this narrative).

Although consisting primarily of British, American, and Canadian troops, the multinational makeup of the Russian Expeditionary Force can be seen in this photograph of soldiers from (l-r) France, America (2), Russia, and Britain, all drawing rations from an Archangel warehouse. (NARS, Still Picture Collection No. 50659)

had run across, and were hilariously chanting a ditty they had improvised, the main theme of which was: "Oh you ruble, oh you kopek."

The 337th Field Hospital went into action right away. The flu epidemic had struck suddenly and with deadly virulence. The Red Cross hospital in Archangel, opened Sept. 10th on Troitsky St., near Olga barracks, was immediately filled, as was the crude Russian hospital at Bakaritza. Several of the rude barracks took over the overflow. Later, during October, a convalescent hospital was opened in an old sailors home in Archangel near American headquarters. In Bakaritza, as else-

A Signal Corps photographic unit accompanied American troops to Archangel, creating a visual record of most aspects of their experience. (NARS, U.S. Army Signal Corps Photograph, no. SC 62503)

where, the medical supplies were exhausted, those available being CCC pills and cathartics only.[12] In the makeshift barracks hospitals in Bakaritza the patients had no beds, but lay on stretchers without mattresses or pillows, lying in their o.d. uniforms with only a single blanket for cover. The place was a bedlam of coughings, hackings, of rasping, stertorous breathings, of moans and incoherent cries, all like some grisly

12. "CCC" refers to Cascarets Candy Cathartic, a popular patent medicine diuretic, hardly the medicine to be using to treat soldiers suffering from flu and diarrhea. Janice Rae McTavish, *Pain and Profits: The History of the Headache and Its Remedies in America* (New Brunswick, NJ: Rutgers University Press, 2004), p. 146.

charnel house. All we could do was to stand and watch some poor fellow, gasping, burning with fever and dripping with sweat, and then a sudden rigidity, an abrupt silence, and the staring eyes became fixed and vacant.

I had just wiped the brow of one struggling patient, and went out to get a fresh pail of water and when I came back shortly after[ward], they were carrying him out. (By the way, there was no well nor pump, so we had to get our drinking water by dipping a pail in the swamp outside. The water was yellow like tea and of course had to be boiled.) I remember one patient, delirious and far gone, had got the idea that we were hiding oranges under his bed and he kept demanding those oranges. As I said before, all we had to give them in the way of medicine was cathartics and consequently the bowel contents were reduced to uncontrollable liquid. The fellow finally gave an ultimatum: "Either give me those oranges before I count three or I'll let her rip." Then "one-two-three" and let her rip he did, and he lay befouled in his own vile and foul smelling excrescence. And immediately after[ward] he gasped out his last breath. One patient, [Jesse] Jackson his name, lay semiconscious on his stretcher, and, apparently haunted by some painful recollection of the past, kept up a continuous agonizing at intervals all throughout the night and which never varied, "Oh God, oh God, oh God." When I came back on duty the next night the stretcher was vacated.

One day I was scheduled for service at the Russian hospital where several Americans had been sent, and I was directed to give an enema to a soldier in pretty bad shape. As a matter of fact we had had practically no training at all in these matters back in Camp Custer; in fact I scarcely knew what an enema was. However, I somehow managed to locate the necessary apparatus, and was struggling to insert the tube in the proper orifice, but without any success. As I wrestled away, the patient, too weak to even move, lay there in a feverish sweat, cursing me with an obscene vocabulary that would have been the envy of a buccaneer of the old Spanish Main. It so happened that one of the Russian nurses, looking in from the hallway in passing, and noticing my predicament, came in and deftly inserted that nozzle with a simple twist of the wrist. The patient, however, did not survive the day.[13]

13. Although now medically discredited, in the early years of the twentieth century, "colon cleansing" with an enema of warm and clear or soapy water — or mineral

When the North Russia Expeditionary Force arrived in Archangel, British officers made this handsome structure their headquarters. The U.S. Army Signal Corps photographer who took the photograph called it the "best building in Archangel." (NARS, U.S. Army Signal Corps Photograph, no. SC 97650-24)

I remember being detailed with another partner to have charge of a ward set up in a room in one of the buildings. The place was absolutely jammed with flu patients lying on the usual stretchers placed on [saw]horses. We arranged between ourselves to work in shifts, one fellow to remain awake and watch for emergencies, the other, in the meantime, sleeping out his shift on the floor behind the stove. Whenever a patient shuffled off his mortal coil, whoever was in charge would wake the other, and between them they would carry out the corpse and store it in the hallway. Sometimes this was difficult, because if the deceased happened to be wedged in some corner it was necessary to lift him across other sleeping patients to get him out. In the morning a detail would come around to the various buildings and pick up the

oil — was a widely practiced procedure to clean and detoxify a patient's bowels. Stephen Barrett, "Gastrointestinal Quackery: Colonics, Laxatives, and More," *Quackwatch* (http://www.quackwatch.org/01QuackeryRelatedTopics/gastro.html).

The U.S. Army 339th Infantry's headquarters company took over this large modern building, which boasted electricity and steam heat, two commodities that were found in only a limited number of Archangel structures. (NARS, U.S. Army Signal Corps Photograph, no. SC 161699)

corpses who had expired during the night; and they were transported to the new American cemetery in Archangel.

Finally, after some hectic weeks the influenza epidemic had run its course, as far as our troops were concerned, but during that time some one hundred boys had died. Fortunately none of the 337th outfit had died, although some had been hit pretty hard and were quite a while in recuperating.[14]

Later in the month our company was split up into two units, designated section A and section B, respectively. At that time Section A was sent up the Dvina to Beresnik and took over a Russian civilian hospital, about a mile to the north. [Anderson's unit was part of Section B.]

14. Anderson's estimate of 100 flu deaths is high. Other sources place the number of deaths from disease at 69, mostly from Spanish flu. In addition to disease, 83 American soldiers died in action, 27 died later from their wounds, 12 died while prisoners of war, 14 died from other causes (mostly accidents), and 29 were reported missing in action. After the war, an American recovery team located 105 bodies in the American cemetery and other Russian sites and returned them to Michigan. Other bodies remain unrecovered. Joel R. Moore, Harry H. Mead, and Lewis E. Jahns, *The History of the American Expedition Fighting the Bolsheviki, Campaigning in North Russia, 1918-1919* (Nashville: Battery Press, 2003; reprint of original 1920 publication).

Archangel

I had once crossed over to Archangel in a motorboat with a couple of comrades shortly after we had arrived here. I remember we had to step over a number of small boats moored alongside the shoreline before reaching terra firma. The streets at that time seemed strangely deserted; perhaps it was Sunday, I don't remember. We came over to the main street which was lined with some quite imposing buildings, impressive architecturally. A line of street car tracks ran along the center of the street, but no cars seemed to be running. It seemed odd to see a good sized flock of goats moving up the main street. One other thing we noticed was the multitude of chimneys protruding from the roofs to give outlet to the great number of brick stoves in each building. Although Archangel is normally a city of some 45,000; at that time it was

The American force's officer corps posed for this photograph in front of their headquarters. Col. George E. Stewart is in the front row, fourth from left.   (NARS, Still Picture Collection No. 50603)

Stevedores using small carts drawn by Russian ponies unloaded cargo intended for troop support.   (NARS, U.S. Army Signal Corps Photograph, no. SC 50609)

estimated (by Gen. [Edmond] Ironside [head of the expeditionary force]) to have 100,000 inhabitants plus 15,000 troops.

Once the crisis at Bakaritza had ended and the 337th was no longer needed there, our outfit, Section B, was moved over to Archangel.

Much of the transportation on the Dvina was by means of barges. These were long, blunt nosed and clumsy and carried various cargoes up and down river — fish, flax, vegetables, cattle, sheep, lumber and hides. The lower hold was dark and damp and stank to high heaven. One of these barges had been requisitioned by the Allies and had been transformed into a hospital ship. The hold had been fumigated and cleaned, the upper deck enclosed. There was a walkway around the side, a kitchen in the rear and a double backhouse protruding over the back end. In the center amid ship, a two story house-like structure with V-roofs and a stairway had been constructed for officer's quarters.

Here we were quartered when we arrived in Archangel and we spread our blankets along both sides of the upper deck. For our chow we had to hike some distance up the street to the north where the Smolney barracks were located. There was a large yard in the rear where a cook shed was, and we ate outdoors from our messkits, sitting on the ground. We did not stay in our present quarters long, for shortly after, arrangements were made for us to move to an upper room in the Smolney barracks. This was a large, handsome brick building with numerous large rooms and wide staircases. Along the walls were hanging

Detailed to establish a receiving and convalescing hospital in an old stone building, Anderson's unit was aided by Bolshevik prisoner work teams, shown here receiving their noon lunch portion of boiled rice from an American guard.   (NARS, U.S. Army Signal Corps Photograph, no. SC 50611)

some elegant oil paintings; one, placed above a staircase, which I especially admired. It depicted a richly furnished apartment; the characters were apparently of the nobility. One figure, richly appareled, as were the others, was fleeing up a stairway, brandishing a bloody knife, having just murdered a distinguished nobleman, who lay surrounded by his appalled and horrified companions.

Soon after this we were put on a special detail. Our Major [Jonas R.] Longely was in charge of renovating a receiving and convalescent hospital. This was in an old but impressive looking structure, with a stone exterior. It had previously been a meteorological institution and was said to be some 200 years old. We began by clearing away the debris that cluttered up the area around it, and taking a cross-cut saw to some old logs and timbers that lay on the premises.

During the days following, a detail armed with rifles went each morning over to the two storied, white stuccoed prison surrounded by a similar white wall 12 or 14 feet high. Here they checked out for us a group of some dozen or more bedraggled looking prisoners, which we herded through the streets to the new projected hospital. Arriving there we split them into groups of three or so, and set each group to sweeping, scrubbing and cleaning out the various rooms. Each one of our detail was in charge of a group, keeping an eye on them with rifle constantly in hand. They certainly were a wretched, miserable looking aggregation. I have no idea what their crimes were; probably they were political prisoners. I, for one, was rather flabbergasted when it came to lunch time. The prison authorities sent over a pail of boiled rice and set it on the floor in the middle of the room and gave each of them a wooden spoon. It was up to them, a dozen or more, to crowd around that pail as best they could to try and get a few spoonfuls before it was all gone. They must all have been half starved all of the time. At one time one of my group had disappeared and I rounded him up on the floor below beneath a kitchen stairway. He had gotten hold of the head of a fish that had been thrown aside and was eating it raw with evident relish. There was one certain prisoner who came every day and whom I particularly noticed. He was rather tall and thin, and wore a long drab-orange coat that extended to his ankles and on his head was one of those gray astrakhan hats. I have never seen a more woe-begone face; he seemed plunged in the very depths of misery. He stood with each hand shoved up a sleeve, never speaking, the very embodiment of hopeless despair. One of our hard-boiled sergeants seemed to see something ludicrous about the poor fellow and referred to him sacrilegiously as "sleeping Jesus."

The view from the upper front windows was superb. The building was situated on a slight eminence overlooking the vast expanse of the lower Dvina. That majestic river extended in both distances as far as the eye could reach, while off to the west Bakaritza and the opposite shore line were barely discernible across the bay, and the setting sun sent an amber glow scintillating across the water. The weather throughout September and early October was still quite mellow and bland.

CHAPTER FOUR

Archangel to Shenkursk

"PEACE HAS COME" declared the *Grand Rapids Herald* on November 11, 1918, announcing that hostilities on World War I's western front had ceased at eleven o'clock in the morning — the "eleventh hour of the eleventh day of the eleventh month." As they read the news, most West Michigan families began counting the days until their family members and friends would return from service with the American Expeditionary Force in Europe.

Unfortunately, for Godfrey Anderson and his compatriots in northern Russia, November 1918 marked the beginning, not the end, of their war. As their political leaders signed peace documents ending the war in western Europe, the Allied members of the North Russia Expeditionary Force began a winter offensive along river and railroad routes that took them deep into the dense swamps and forests south of Archangel. Allied soldiers moved south along three separate routes, determined not only to drive Bolshevik forces back toward St. Petersburg and Moscow, but also to meet the Czech Legion, which was making its way from the east, and to provide support to anti-Bolshevik forces, which Western leaders hoped would establish a more moderate, democratically elected government in Russia.

The advance out of Archangel was a bold plan initiated by General Frederick C. Poole, and it had some initial success when the Bolshevik forces fell back rather than becoming engaged in large-scale battles. But Poole had neither sufficient troops and materials nor the leadership qualities for long-term success. For each *verst* (a Russian measurement equivalent to 3,500 feet, about two-thirds of a mile) that his troops pushed south, their supply line became longer and more vulnerable, and their defensive perimeter became more porous. They also found themselves in an increasingly inhospitable environment, one that their opponents understood far better than they did. While the Allied troops — primarily Americans and Canadians — were scurrying to find suitable winter quarters and planning to wait out the harsh weather as comfortably as possible, their adversaries were laying plans for a winter offensive. It was not a good scenario, and General Poole did not appreciate the predicament he had created.

As he planned the offensive, General Poole divided the hospital unit into two groups to accompany the assault up the Dvina River toward the Vaga River, and up the Vologda railroad line. He assigned Anderson's group to the Dvina assault. Those on the railroad line took hospital cars with them, but on the river there were only the simple structures of small villages. Villagers generally offered assistance to the Americans, and even socialized with them on occasion. The *New York Times* reported that the soldiers' kindnesses often won over villagers, and Anderson recalls a dance in which local residents joined the Americans.[1] The Americans settled in along their front, and despite constant skirmishing with Bolshevik patrols, expected only limited action until spring.

The relative calm lasted only until early January 1919, when a heavy artillery bombardment from guns the Bolsheviks had brought up over the frozen ground signaled the beginning of a winter offensive by the Red fighters, who were determined to retake the land they had lost.

"Ordered off on a new adventure . . ."

We got the place pretty well cleaned up but did not remain in Archangel long enough to see Major Longely get established there (it was opened Nov. 22), for we were ordered off on a new adventure. It was

1. *New York Times*, October 7, 1918.

sometime during early October that the 337th Field Hospital Section B again set up quarters aboard the hospital barge mentioned before (the *Michigan* she had been dubbed); and not long after a tug appeared and attached a line to our bow. Presently we began to move slowly upstream toward an area of which then we knew absolutely nothing.

From Archangel to Beresnik

The province of Archangel lies in the northernmost part of European Russia, beginning above and extending south of the Arctic Circle. It is mostly densely forested, interspersed by a number of lakes. The area is marshy in places as this part of Russia was, geologically speaking, but recently elevated above the sea; and the area is largely tundra. Only about 2% of the area is arable, or fit for cultivation, and the average population of the province is about two to the square mile. The Dvina is the largest river in the province, and is formed by the junction of the Suhona and Vychegada [Yug] rivers at Kotlas, a little over 300 miles from Archangel. Its three main tributaries are the Pinega, the Emtsa and the Vaga rivers, the [first] some 75 miles, the second some 95 miles, and the third some 155 miles from Archangel, as the aeroplane flies. There is but one railroad, which runs straight south 400 miles from Bakaritza to Vologda, a town of some 50,000 inhabitants. Here one branch runs some 275 miles [west] to Petrograd and the other continues about the same distance [southeast] to Moscow.[2]

The climate in winter is severe; the area is covered with deep snow and the river is frozen for nearly six months. The ice in the river and the bay of Archangel and the White Sea averages fifteen feet thick. The temperature during the coldest months averages around forty below zero, but because it remains so constant one is not as aware of it as

2. Czar Peter the Great founded St. Petersburg in 1703, and nine years later he made it his country's capital, supplanting Moscow. With the start of World War I, the name St. Petersburg sounded too German to Russia's leaders, and in 1914 they renamed the city Petrograd. In early 1918, during the Russian civil war, the city's proximity to the border and anti-Soviet armies caused the Bolsheviks to transfer the capital to Moscow. On January 24, 1924, three days after Lenin's death, Petrograd was renamed Leningrad to honor the founder of the Soviet Union. Following the demise of the Soviet Union in 1989, voters chose to restore the name St. Petersburg.

Allied leaders used British airplanes equipped with pontoons in the warm months and skis in winter to gather intelligence about Bolshevik troop movements.   (NARS, Still Picture Collection, no. 89956)

if it fluctuated from time to time.[3] Distances are measured by versts, each verst equal to about two thirds of a mile or 1.067 kilo[meter]s.

For the first fifty miles or so the Dvina takes a southeasterly course. During this part of its course the river is studded with numerous islands and a half dozen or so are very large, in places five or six miles between opposite shores. At Kotlas the river swings to the south for some eighty miles, then reverts to the southeast again to its termination. The Dvina compares favorably in size to the lower Mississippi and has virtually no banks to retrain it in its course, and consequently,

3. Modern weather data clarify Anderson's memory of Archangel's cold winter weather. According to the official weather Web site of the BBC, between November and March, the city's average temperatures range from highs between 10° and 28° F and lows from minus 4° to minus 20° F. Temperature extremes range from lows of -40° F to highs of 40° F. Summer temperatures rise to 50-70° F in July. For three months, November to February, the region receives little more than three hours of measurable sunlight per day; but it enjoys more than twenty-one hours of sunlight per day at its June-July peak (*BBC* Weather, Average Conditions, http://www.bbc.co.uk/weather/world/city_guides/results.shtml?tt=TT004410).

especially during high water, it meanders widely over the surrounding country, constantly creating new channels.

The next two weeks were a time of grateful relaxation. There were no roll calls or setting up exercises. The officers remained in their second story sanctum sanctorum; the sergeants occupied another quarter and rarely showed up, and we were left largely to our own devices. We reclined on our pallets strung along the sides of our vessel, smoking the cigarettes issued by the Red Cross or other organizations. We discovered a phonograph in the hold along with some records; one, I remember, played constantly and went, "The bells are ringing for me and my Gal, etc."[4] And there were boxes of books there, too. I got hold of Crane's "Red Badge of Courage" and Mary Johnston's "To Have and to Hold."[5] We managed to locate some large slab of chocolate two inches thick. There had been crates of canned peaches, pears, plums and the like, but the officers had managed to appropriate all these. Also stored below was a great number of second hand disassembled iron bunks which the major had rounded up somewhere. These were designed to be hooked together in pairs, upper and lower, and attached to another pair at the ends, for as far as room permitted. There was a passageway around the rear half of the barge where we were quartered, where we could stroll about and enjoy the scenery. We lined up for our chow in the cook shed at the rear, and as said before there was a double backhouse protruding over the end of the barge. Towed by a rope from the rear was a dinghy with a canvas awning and filled with straw and unoccupied. It was a diversion to somehow scramble aboard this craft and loll there for a couple of hours in grateful privacy. Up ahead the tug wheezed and struggled as it bucked the current while towing the clumsy monstrosity behind it.

The weather was delightful, not cold at all for October, and the scenery was impressive, with dense conifer forests lining the banks, the

4. Published in 1917, "For Me and My Gal" (words by Edgar Leslie and E. Ray Goetz, music by Geo. W. Meyer) was an instant hit.

5. Godfrey Anderson's interest in history carried over to his fiction reading. Stephen Crane's well-known 1895 novel *The Red Badge of Courage* is the story of a young recruit in the American Civil War confronting the cruelty of war. Less well known today, but hugely popular at the time of its publication, Mary Johnston's *To Have and To Hold* is a historical romance novel set in early Virginia.

channels skirting wooded islands, the pink glow of dawn, and finally the setting sun swinging low over the vast majestic panorama. Sometimes there was the soft patter of rain on the roof. In places the current was swifter and the going was tougher and at one time two tugs were attached to the barge to battle against the increased pressure. Every day or so the tug would pull up to a refueling place, where great woodpiles were stacked along the river bank, and we were rousted out to wrestle wood aboard the tug. About this time the officers decided we should post a guard, and one of our compatriots, in turn, would stand in the door with a rifle. Sometimes he would playfully challenge one of us, pointing that rifle dead center. Some of these men were but green neophytes when it came to handling firearms; some probably never had held a rifle before (the medical corps were not issued rifles until later). Some actually had the safety catch off and it is a wonder they did not inadvertently blow someone's head off.

About this time it was reported that someone had stolen the captain's side arm. There was a cursory investigation and some questioning without result. It was some two months later during the week when I was barracks custodian that I chanced to run across the gun carefully concealed among the blankets in the bunk of one of those dubious recruits from the Chicago area. However I did not feel called upon to disclose the whereabouts of the purloined weapon.

At intervals we passed rude villages clustered near the banks and sometimes when we stopped for refueling we were offered "yestels" (eggs) or undersized potatoes (they did not grow large this far north) for sale. The peasants live under a sort of communal system. Around each village are patches of arable land, where each family had a portion allotted to it and for which they are responsible. The crops are mostly immature and undersized and consist chiefly of oats, flax, rye and some buckwheat and also there are some turnips, cabbages and a few potatoes. They live mostly on these vegetables, plus a kind of black bread made from rye, a cabbage soup, and more or less on salted fish. Some keep a few chickens which supply some eggs and occasional meat. In season there are wild berries and mushrooms. There is plenty of wild game too, rabbits, quails and grouse and there are great numbers of wild ducks. The swamps abound with cranberries.

In the long winter months the women spin thread from the flax

Because they retained a steady heat level for long periods of time, huge Russian stoves not only heated homes but also provided heat for meal preparation and baking. This stove was kept constantly active heating, baking, and cooking at the American Red Cross Hospital. (NARS, U.S. Army Signal Corps Photograph, no. SC 161721)

and weave cloth. In each house is the usual brick stove to which is connected their prized possession, the samovar, which always contains hot water for their tea.[6] The men spend most of their time in winter relaxing on top of the stove.[7] In every peasant home there is the same identical disagreeable stench, the cause of which I could never determine, whether from the salted fish or fish oil or flax or the general lack of ventilation in sealing everything to shut out the bitter cold. By the way, there were plenty of cockroaches, cooties and bedbugs.

6. Samovars are metal water heaters crafted of copper, brass, bronze, or tin, often trimmed with silver, gold, and nickel, with a faucet near the bottom and a metal heating pipe running vertically through the middle. When filled with burning coal or charcoal, the pipe heats water in the surrounding container. Newer samovars generally use electricity. Many samovars have an attachment on the tops of their lids where a teapot used to brew a strong tea concentrate is heated.

7. Russian stoves, which feature a small firebox surrounded by a large brick-walled flue chambers, are exceptionally efficient heating devices. Heat from the firebox is absorbed into the stove's brick walls and from there slowly radiates into the room. Because the stoves cool slowly, they require fueling only two or three times a day and can efficiently heat a 400-square-foot area (*The Russian Stove: Simple Technology Providing Maximum Efficiency*, http://www.russianstove.com).

The ongoing war was difficult for small Russian communities inland from Archangel, and villagers regularly showed up at the barracks and mess halls seeking food. This photo shows American soldiers saving a portion of their meal to share.   (NARS, Still Picture Collection No. 89977)

Beresnik

Well anyway, those two weeks we spent bucking our way up the Dvina — the most pleasant we were to experience in North Russia for a long time — finally came to an end. We reached Beresnik around the 16th or 17th of October and tied up at a wharf there on the west bank. Beresnik is about 150 miles from Archangel. It occupies two different locations. The first is along the river where some two dozen shacks, rude buildings and warehouses, are lined along the shore for half a mile or so. The other location lies nearly half a mile from the river on higher ground. The area between is a low flat plain and uninhabited, probably communal land, fenced in here and there. There is a magnificent cathedral in the upper town. About the same distance north of the village was located the Russian hospital, now occupied by Section A of the 337th Field Hospital. That comprised neat, one story buildings, clapboard sided and painted a battleship gray with white trim, with several outhouses in the rear.

Shortly after we had arrived here a hospital boat called the *Currier* arrived at Beresnik from the Dvina front farther upstream with some wounded Royal Scots destined for the hospital. These were transported on whatever rude carts were available, but a few were so painfully injured that they would not be able to stand the rude jolting over the rough terrain. For each of these eight medics were detailed to carry him shoulder high on stretchers to the hospital mentioned above. These worked in shifts, four carrying for a while, then relieved by the other four at intervals. The patient was a bit apprehensive that we might stumble and fall and he be thrown to the ground, an agonizing prospect for him, but we delivered him safe and sound to intensive care. We remained in Beresnik only two or three days.

Beresnik to Shenkursk

After this short stopover at Beresnik, Section B of the 337th was transferred to the *Currier,* a sidewheeler, along with medical and Red Cross supplies, and of course all those bothersome iron bunks mentioned before. The hospital barge, the *Michigan,* which we now abandoned, was to be used as a convalescent ship in charge of the British R.A.M.C. There were also some refugees and a few prisoners aboard the *Currier.*

Some six or seven miles above Beresnik we entered one of the main tributaries of the Dvina, the Vaga, whose general course is almost exactly due south, but unlike the Dvina, which flows in a steady course with few convolutions, the course of the Vaga is serpentine and tortuous, full of loops, windings, reversals and contortions like those of some wounded snake in death throes. The Vaga is narrower but its current is more rapid than that of the Dvina, it is less encumbered with islands, and is more or less lined with bluffs from fifty to a hundred feet high on either side. Its scenery is more varied and interesting. We passed more villages on this route than on that of the Dvina, and most of them were larger and less primitive looking.[8]

8. The Vaga River is the Dvina's largest tributary. It is 358 miles long, drains a

The typical villages of North Russia are usually but a cluster of rude, unpainted, weatherbeaten log structures, but in the midst of every village or hamlet, however rude or insignificant, there is the ubiquitous church, painted white with green roof and surmounted by one or more onion domed steeples in the Orthodox style, towering above all the other buildings.

Our bunks were below the water line. I remember I could reach out the port hole while still reclining and wash off my mess-kit in the water rushing by.

We were told later that it was against the rules of the Russian river crews to travel by night and that it had been necessary to force them into complying. We were ordered to post guards at night to guard both the stores and the prisoners, etc. I remember I was detailed to stand guard on one end of the roof with a companion at the other end, ostensibly to watch that sparks from the smokestack didn't set fire to the ship. That was a spooky experience. The night with its pale, ghostly moonlight, the dark and brooding forests and bluffs looming along either shore, the shadowy, mystic windings of the river, from that elevated perch gave one an eerie feeling as of penetrating some accursed and god-forsaken wilderness.

One of the prisoners, suspected of being a spy, tried to escape through a window but was caught before he could make his get-away.

Shenkursk

We arrived at Shenkursk about noon the next day. This town is some 65 miles from Beresnik and about 200 miles in a direct line from Archangel. We could not see anything of the town from the steamer because there was a high, sloping wooded bluff extending all along that side of the river, that hid the town. However, we soon were put to work toting all our paraphernalia, including all those iron bunks mentioned before, up a road that wound to the top of the bluff. There we got our view of Shenkursk, a town that will go down in American and Michigan history. It was the second largest town in the Archangel District

---

17,000-square-mile basin, and generally freezes in mid-November and does not thaw until mid-April (http://en.wikipedia.org/wiki/Vaga_River).

with a population of several thousand, it is said, although the streets seemed largely deserted at the time.[9]

Shenkursk's limits extended perhaps half a mile from east to west and the same from north to south, or perhaps a bit farther. Troitsa was the main thoroughfare running east and west and running a bit more along the eastern edge of the town, with a number of mercantile establishments mostly along the east side of the street, which had been cleaned out by the fleeing Reds. The south end of the street wound down the bluff to the river landing while the other end continued past a monastery, beyond which it degenerated into a rude trail that lost itself in the dense forest beyond. It is headed toward Seltso, some forty miles distant but rarely traveled beyond a wretched village called Kodima, about half that distance. At the southeast end of the town, near the bluff over the river, stood a great church almost square in shape, white stuccoed, its outlines rather severe and plain, but surmounted by five turnip shaped domes, the center one taller and larger, all of a greenish tint, which reflected a scintillating luster when the sunlight struck them.

At the other end of the street was the huge monastery, surrounded by a high wall, all stuccoed with a white plaster — a brooding, gloomy, somewhat repellent looking place, almost like a walled-in prison. Somewhat to the right of this was a hospital set within the fringe of the surrounding forest. There were various types of buildings in the town — log, frame buildings with siding or part siding, some brick. Some were touched up in the gables with an ochre paint, some had weather vanes with the usual rooster. There were Russian barracks, a saw mill, and a printing shop among others. (I remember that a day or so after the armistice in France on Nov. 11, this printing shop put out on a large sheet the news of, and the entire terms of, the armistice. I was presented a copy; it was printed in Russian. I am still wondering how in the world they got this scoop so quickly on this remote frontier and from such a distance.)

The high school or college, whatever it was, was a large two-storied rectangular building set back some 200 feet from a street run-

9. Situated on the right bank of the Vaga River, Shenkursk, with a current population of slightly more than 6,000, is the administrative center of Shenkursky District of the Archangelsk Oblast. It began as a small trading town named Vaga in the fourteenth century. Catherine the Great chartered the town as Shenkursk in 1780 (http://www.nationmaster.com/encyclopedia/Shenkursk).

Until the troops retreated from the small city, this two-story wooden structure served as the headquarters for those stationed in and around Shenkursk. (NARS, U.S. Army Signal Corps Photograph, no. SC 152812)

ning at right angles and west of Troitsa Street. It was a handsome frame structure with a narrow siding painted a blue-gray with white trim, with outhouses at the rear. There was a wide entrance at the front, facing which, at the back was a stairway leading to the upper floor. A large room extended along the entire front of the upper floor and had a grand piano and an artificial palm. This room became the main ward of the hospital. There were many other rooms in the building; some were used as wards when there was an overflow of patients. The officer's quarters were also on the second floor as was the kitchen in the rear, and a mess hall was set up in a room just below. The sergeants also had their private quarters.

There was a large attic which I later managed to explore, in which was stored a large number of textbooks. Being in Russian I could not make them out, except that by the mathematical symbols and diagrams in some, I deduced they were algebras, geometries, trigonometries, etc. This building was taken over by Section B of the 337th for a permanent field hospital.

The grounds surrounding the building were spacious, especially at the rear, where there was a large number of tall spruces resting on the ground, it seemed. The sides and rear of the grounds were enclosed by a fence of upright boards. Beyond the fence and to the right there was a large two-story building that came right up to the street and which was subsequently taken over by the 337th for a secondary or convalescent hospital. Transit between the two buildings was established by knocking a couple of boards out of the fence. At the left and also coming up to the street was another dwelling of three or four rooms both up and down, the upper floor of which was taken over for a barracks for the corporals and buck privates. Here were hooked up some of those iron bunks, uppers and lowers, that we had hauled all the way from

Archangel. There was one of those brick stoves set in the center of the house so that part of it protruded into each of the four rooms. There was a privy off the stairway where the excrescence dropped two stories into a dung pile, where it froze immediately so there were no odors, and it was simply hauled out on the fields just before the spring thaws.

As said before, the main building was set back a hundred feet or more from the street, and in this front yard were set up some simple meteorological devices, where a professor of the school came every day to check them. There was a well with a windlass about half way between our barracks and the main hospital, a barn in the rear, also a bath house or sauna.

Beyond the street, across from the main building was an extensive field of several acres, with a row of buildings along the far side. Here the Cossack cavalry would sometimes drill and maneuver. The street in front of our barracks sloped a bit to the east where, almost hid by the encroaching forest, although only a block away, was another attractive brick structure that looked like an official building of some kind.

All in all, Shenkursk was a higher class place than the more or less squalid villages we had so far encountered. It lay high, was a healthy place, located on sandy ground, well drained, and the people seemed more prosperous and better educated than most. It was surrounded on three sides by dense forests with swamps here and there. Standing atop the bluff and looking off to the south beyond the river was a low lying practically treeless plain stretching off to infinity, it seemed. Far to the southwest could be discerned the village of Nikolaievskaya with its domed church, and way off to the left lay another miserable cluster of shacks too insignificant to deserve a name. The river could be seen below coming and going, curving around the bluff.

As soon as we had got ourselves established in our new quarters we were set to moving various articles and paraphernalia belonging to the school over to hospital #2 and storing them in a room there. I remember one of the articles I carried was a complete female skeleton wired together and mounted on a stand. The remainder of those iron bunks were stored in a small stone hut behind our barracks and guards were placed there all night in two hour shifts. Two k.p.'s were appointed each week; the most grueling part of their job was to carry water by the pail from the well up a flight of stairs to the kitchen in the back, a seemingly endless job. The chow had to be carried downstairs to the

mess hall; then came the drudgery of scraping pans and dixies and lug-
ging up the supplies the mess sergeant brought over.

The people of Shenkursk were hostile to the Bolsheviks and the
revolution itself and many refugees found shelter here; and when the
British and Americans arrived at Beresnik to prepare for their expedition up the Dvina, a delegation from Shenkursk arrived at headquarters to urge [them to] help to protect their town from the Reds, who
were assembling in large numbers in the area around Vologda.[10] Consequently on the 15th of September, Capt. [Otto] Odjard and Lieutenant [Harry] Mead, with a platoon of Co. A, went up the river by
steamer, accompanied by a gunboat, and arrived at Shenkursk two days
later. They took possession of the town by default, as the Bolos had left
without firing a shot, after looting the town, as said before.[11] The
American troops were well received by the citizens, and they found
themselves installed in comfortable barracks and imagined they were
sitting pretty for the winter. However, they were soon disillusioned, for
shortly after[ward] they received news that British staff officers, with a
great stock of supplies and a number of garrison soldiers were on their
way to stay at Shenkursk, while Company A was ordered to proceed up
the river to contact the enemy.

They went up in the steamer *Tolstoy*. At a village named Gorks
they ran into fire and immediately landed and pursued the enemy on
land. Abandoning the steamer they proceeded on foot under wretched
conditions, traveling through woods and swampy terrain, wet and bedraggled, short of rations, without overcoats and plagued with swollen
feet; they continued on for a week until they reached the village of
Puya. This was the farthest south any unit was ever to reach. Here they
ran into a large enemy force, while another detachment blocked their
rear. However, they inflicted a severe defeat upon the enemy, killing

10. The administrative center of the Vologda Oblast, with a 2002 population of
nearly 300,000, Vologda, which takes its name from the river that flows through the
city, had a population of about 30,000 at the beginning of World War I. It lies about
250 miles due south of Archangel (*All-Russia Population Census of 2002*, Federal State
Statistics Service, 2007: http://perepis2002.ru/ct/html/TOM_01_04_1.htm; http://
en.wikipedia.org/wiki/Vologda).

11. "Bolos" is the nickname the Allied troops gave the Bolshevik soldiers they encountered in Russia.

In addition to commandeering buildings to serve as hospitals, barracks, warehouses, and head-quarters, engineers with the American troops hastily built a group of barracks they dubbed Camp Michigan.　(NARS, U.S. Army Signal Corps Photograph, no. SC 50614)

fifty while only four of their number were wounded, and managed to retreat back to Rovdino, about thirty miles south of Shenkursk. Here they remained about two weeks. On October 18th they moved back to the village of Ust Padenga, about fifteen miles from Shenkursk, where they now set up their winter quarters.

And now there began a great activity in the strengthening of the defenses of Shenkursk. A detachment of the 310th Engineers arrived there. Indeed these had units on all fronts wherever their services were needed. They began to construct block houses, string barbed wire, dig trenches and prepare dugouts. It was said that in Archangel they even ran the street cars, operated saw mills, the waterworks, and the Archangel power plant, built barracks, a wireless station and much more.

One day my buddy and I happened to stroll over to the big cathedral atop the river bluff. The engineers were digging a trench along the bluff near the church overlooking that wide expanse stretching off beyond the river. (They later built a dugout adjoining the trench and installed a sheet iron stove in it.) They evidently had run into an ancient cemetery adjacent to the church, for atop the ridge of dirt thrown up by them were a number of human skulls and bones they had excavated. One such skull was lying conveniently at hand, its eye sockets full of frozen mud. With something of the compulsion of schoolboys to idly kick a tin can ahead of them down the street, we thoughtlessly propelled poor Yorick ahead of us down Troitsa Street through town until we finally abandoned it somewhere along the roadway.

About this time a few of our men were detailed to go down to the river landing to guard a steamer that had just come in. It was a British boat, I believe. Anyway, those guards came back with a sizable amount of rum, stout and ale, and later got themselves pretty well inebriated. I remember the night of Thanksgiving, especially. The cooks had come up with a special dinner that day, and some of the boys had hit the bottle again, and heaved up that dinner over the floor and on themselves and lay snoring enveloped in their own vomit.[12]

Our first snowfall came during the last week in October, but by November it had all disappeared and the ground was as soft and muddy as ever. It got dark earlier but otherwise so far the weather was not much different than it was back home. Although ice was forming on the river by the 1st of November boats were running as late as the 5th, because at 8 o'clock that night one [P]rivate Nelson and myself were detailed to go down to the river with a British officer to carry up his baggage. When we got back they were just handing out the mail, which presumably had come in on the same boat. Believe me, there was great excitement when the mail came in. All evening the fellows were lying on their bunks deeply absorbed in news from home. There had been a wood-cutting gang out all day, some distance from the barracks. The wood was hauled back on a couple of machine-gun car-

---

12. The *New York Times* reported a somewhat different version of the soldiers' 1918 Thanksgiving observance. The newspaper reported that "in box cars, block houses, village billets and birch bough shelters, and around camp fires near the Bolshevist lines," the troops did their best "to observe an old-fashioned American Thanksgiving." In addition to special rations for the occasion, troops received a proclamation from DeWitt C. Poole Jr. of the U.S. embassy at Archangel declaring "the necessity of their remaining in Russia until the job was finished and calling attention to the importance of the task" (*New York Times*, Nov. 29, 1918).

riages picked up somewhere. We got orders to be prepared to go down to the river at some time later that night to unload a number of wounded coming downstream.

There was in the hospital at this time a Norwegian named Hersted, attached to the Canadian artillery. He had been on the Western front since 1915 and was in the first gas attack that the Kraut[s] launched at Ypres. You could still see its effect on him by his breathing and voice. Once when holding three horses, a shell exploded and killed all three horses but left him practically unscathed. He was now laid up with high fever and rheumatism in a leg.

At this time the woman who had commanded the famous Legion of Death arrived in town.[13]

It was about this time that the flu epidemic hit the Russians, which soon reached appalling virulence.[14] The Russians seemed to have no resistance whatsoever. By the 11th of November [1918, the date of the Armistice] we had around 100 patients on our hands; both our hospitals were filled, as was the Russian civilian hospital. The small stone hut at the rear of our barracks was full of corpses awaiting coffins, of which there was a shortage. It was the same in the outlands — people

13. Women combatants participated on both sides during World War I. One of the most interesting groups was the organization called the "Legia Smirti," or Legion of Death, composed of trained women soldiers recruited from all classes. Brought together in 1917 by twenty-seven-year-old Maria Bochkareva, the unit fought in several engagements against the Germans. Following especially hard action near Smorgon, in Belarus, in July 1917, the women were sent to a camp back of the lines on the northern front. When they took over the Russian government, Bolshevik leaders disbanded the women's legion. Bochkareva is thought to have stayed in the north, where Godfrey Anderson learned of her presence. Bolshevik leaders arrested her as a White Russian leader in 1919, and she was executed by firing squad on May 16, 1920. *The Illustrated War News*, London, August 8, 1917; reprinted in "The Great War in a Different Light" (http://www.greatwardifferent.com/Great_War/Women_Warriors/.htm). See also Laurie Stoff, *They Fought for the Motherland: Russia's Women Soldiers in World War I and the Revolution* (Lawrence: University Press of Kansas, 2006).

14. Perhaps because it was sparsely populated and isolated, the Archangelsk Oblast had avoided the initial flu outbreak, but the British and American soldiers brought the disease ashore with them, where it spread quickly in close and generally unsanitary living conditions (Joel R. Moore, Harry H. Mead, and Lewis E. Jahns, *The History of the American Expedition Fighting the Bolsheviki* [Detroit, 1920], p. 67).

Maria Bochkareva was quite likely the woman soldier Anderson mentions in his memoir. Following the Bolshevik takeover, she fled to the United States, but returned to Archangel in August 1918 and resumed her organizing efforts until arrested by Bolshevik authorities in 1919. A Bolshevik firing squad executed her in 1920. (Library of Congress, George Grantham Bain Collection, http://hdl.loc.gov/loc.pnp/ggbain.26866)

dying by the hundreds. Funeral processions were constantly wailing through the streets.

I happened to be looking out of an upstairs window facing the yard at the west side of the building. There were two Russian corpses laid out side by side on the lids of their coffins, which were set on wooden horses. The two lay there with faces exposed, ghastly and gruesome. Presently a procession appeared led by a couple of Orthodox priests with profuse black whiskers and arrayed in gaudy robes, each swinging a smoking censer. Accompanying them were a group of females, the equivalent of nuns, I suppose. The priests began a lugubrious chant in a deep basso. At intervals the females came in with a high pitched doleful interlude. Then there were some unintelligible (to me) incantations, after which the corpses were carried away, probably to the cathedral, where I am told, during the chants and the services, every member of the funeral party kissed a crucifix held by the priest.

Even when the epidemic had passed its climax, patients were steadily coming in during the rest of the year. We had from time to time several different undertakers detailed for that duty. Back in Bakaritza he would set the corpse up against the wall and shave him; with the Russians this detail was dispensed with because of the luxurious hair that covered most of the face. The main procedure was to tie off the penis and to plug with gauze the throat and anus. The undertaker carried a whittled pine stick for the plugging operation. One of our undertakers was "Pork" Nordman, and when a Russian was momentarily expected to give up the ghost, and especially if it was late at night, he would pace impatiently in the hallway outside the door with the plugging stick behind his ear, and profanely importune the unconscious patient to hurry it up and quit stalling. Another assistant, one Roy Carnes, in working on a corpse, found his plugging stick too thick, and took out his army issued heavy duty jackknife and began shaving it down, smeared as it was by the raw sienna hued excrescence. After a cursory wipe off he stuck the knife back in his pocket. Later that night when he went to the kitchen for a late snack he took out the same jackknife and began peeling an onion for his sandwich. He was later kidded plenty about it. Our first mortician, a fellow called "Shep," lost his job because of purloining valuables from the pockets of the deceased.

It was rather late one night in early December and we were lolling about in our bunks smoking cigarettes, writing letters, engaged in idle chit-chat, not quite ready to turn in, when a corporal came in, carrying a lantern. He came to pick a few men for a special detail. Our assignment was to carry some two or three Russian soldiers, who had died of the flu in our hospital, over to the Russian morgue, some half mile or so away. These corpses were lying in our little stone morgue, each on a stretcher and covered with an o.d. blanket. We started out in a sort of procession, one man at each end of a stretcher, the Corporal (Hart) carrying the lantern. It was a cold wintry night, a heavy snow was falling and a brisk wind blowing in gusts. I was on the tail end of the last stretcher, and the wind kept whipping up the end of the blanket, and exposing a pair of bare feet almost in my face. I had no free arm to fasten the blanket, and so had no alternative but to endure the unpleasant proximity of corns, bunions and jagged toenails all the rest of the way. This gruesome procession turned into the main street along which we now proceeded. Luckily the street was practically deserted because of the weather. We continued to the northeast end of town where the Russian hospital was located at the fringe of the forest.

The place was dark, and repeated poundings brought no response; so we proceeded on to their morgue, which lay farther back in the woods. This place, fairly large, was dark also and as we opened the door we almost stumbled over a scantily dressed corpse lying in the passageway, partly blocking the entrance. We stepped over this grisly impediment and entered the building. There were two good sized rooms, the first apparently crowded with cadavers occupying every inch of space, some lying on the floor, some on stretchers, a few in rude coffins on [saw]horses. We squeezed past a coffin wherein lay an old woman staring with open eyes into space. None of the corpses were covered at all, their faces ghastly and horrible with all manner of bizarre expressions. We passed into the inner room and managed to find a place to deposit our stretchers on the floor. The lantern cast an eerie light over that repellent assemblage, some barely discernible in the shadowy corners. It gave one a feeling of revulsion and horror. The moaning of the wind all around us and the groaning of the limbs in the trees overhead only added to the spookiness of that horrible charnel house. We got out of that place in a hurry and returned to the welcome conviviality of our quarters.

A couple of days later a fellow from Muskegon, one Olson and myself were detailed to go over to this Russian morgue and of all things, just to put two dead soldiers in their coffins. However, this was in the daytime and not quite as eerie as at night. We lifted them into their coffins and tucked an army o.d. blanket around each and tapped on the lids. The top sergeant bawled us out later for not bringing back the blankets, "Dead men don't need no blankets," he informed us.

By the middle of November the ground was covered with snow and the river frozen and navigation came to an end. The sun would come up for a few hours each day, creating a sort of hazy glow as it moved in a short arc far beyond the horizon. One had a feeling of being completely isolated from the rest of the world.

Inside a dugout built to hold off Bolshevik attacks and winter's cold, soldiers wear some of their recently issued winter clothing: woolen socks and sweaters, sleeveless leather jerkins, and leather-soled, felt-lined Shackleton boots of white canvas. (NARS, Still Picture Collection, no.161115)

We had been issued our winter clothing — two suits of winter underwear, heavy knee length woolen socks and sweaters. There was a sleeveless leather jerkin, a fur lined head-dress of white canvas that could be turned down over the neck and ears and tied by a tape under the chin, a long ankle length sheepskin lined overcoat of a dull ochre-orange color with a high turn-up collar, and a pair of Shackleton boots of white canvas, leather soled, felt lined and extending half way to the knees and fastened by a white tape wound about the leg and tied.[15] We kept these boots in reserve, preferring the less clumsy hobnailed boots for the time being, the snow, when it came, being powdery and dry and never wet. In addition to the regular woolen mittens we were issued a pair of deep oversized mittens which were suspended from the shoulders like a harness, whose function was to provide something in which to thrust the hands to keep them warm in the frigid air when traveling.

Shenkursk and its three forward defenses, Visorka Gora, Nijni Gora and Ust Padenga, some fifteen miles upstream, lay in a precarious position. They were located far to the south of the other two fronts on either side, fifty miles beyond Toulgas on Dvina and some eighty miles beyond Verst 445 on the railroad front. Shenkursk was therefore flanked in both directions by the enemy and rumors were rife that the Bolos were collecting an overwhelming force in this area, only waiting for the trails to become frozen and sufficiently hard before launching an attack on Shenkursk. By the middle of November the enemy was becoming increasingly active. On the seventeenth a small [Allied] patrol was ambushed some five or six miles below Ust Padenga, but escaped.

On November 29th, the day after Thanksgiving, Lieut. Francis Cuff of Co. C left Ust Padenga early in the morning with a strong patrol of around one hundred men to rout the enemy from his advanced position in the vicinity. A heavy snow had fallen and the temperature was around twenty degrees below zero. The only trail in this direction led through the forest and at its densest part, not far from the river they were suddenly ambushed by an overwhelming force concealed in the woods. In a moment the forest was swarming with the enemy.

15. Famed explorer Sir Ernest Shackleton had been designated "staff officer in charge of arctic equipment" for the North Russia Expeditionary Force. He selected fur coats, hats and gloves, and fur-lined sleeping bags that were well received, but his felt, canvas-covered "Shackleton" boots, with their smooth leather soles, were another matter. Intended for use with skis, they were warm, but useless on packed snow or ice. Metal studs made the boots more effective on ice and hard-packed snow, but their lack of waterproofing meant that they quickly absorbed water and became cold and sodden when the spring thaw arrived (Clifford Kinvig, *Churchill's Crusade: The British Invasion of Russia, 1918-1920* [London: Hambledon Continuum, 2006], pp. 119-20).

Lieutenant Cuff managed to extricate his platoon except for one detachment which was pinned down at the fringe of the forest near the Vaga. The lieutenant, with a few men, returned to aid them and became separated from the rest and completely surrounded by the enemy. Here he was badly wounded, as were some of his men. Nevertheless they fought fiercely, much like Custer at the Little Big Horn, but all were finally annihilated.

When their bodies were recovered the next day (to be removed to Shenkursk) there was a ring of enemy dead all around them, attesting to the ferocity of their last stand. The enemy had severed the officer's arms and legs, as one report has it. However, there is another version. There was a special funeral ceremony for Lieut. Cuff, which all the military units in the area attended. As we were lined up in the street in front of our barracks, the Captain [Howard Kinyon] made a short speech. The enemy, he said, were castrating the wounded while they were still alive, when Lieut. Cuff pulled out his revolver and shot himself. "That is the kind of enemy you are fighting," he concluded.

Our company then marched at attention to the main street, where many different units were lined up in full dress, all standing at attention. There were British and American companies, Russian enlisted units, a Royal Scot company wearing their bonnets, a Canadian artillery unit, and a company of Cossack cavalry in their flamboyant trappings, among others.

Presently from the great white monastery there came the horse-drawn gun carriage on which was fastened the raw pine casket containing the body of the brave Lieut. Cuff. On top of the casket was his steel helmet. The whole procession marched to the eastern outskirts of the town where a grave had been dug amid a scattering of tall pines at the fringe of the dense forest. All the different military units were deployed in formation on all sides. The casket was then carried to the grave and lowered by ropes, all amid profound silence. There were tributes spoken and then the crash of a firing squad, which echoed and re-echoed through the boundless forest, and finally the melancholy notes of the bugler playing taps. The whole event was profoundly impressive, the snow blanketed terrain, the gloomy environment, the brooding pines bending beneath the weight of their burden of snow, the bitter cold.

The weather every day was getting colder, snow was falling constantly now, the days growing shorter and darker. Frostbites were common. Company C was relieved by Company A on the first of December. They alternated at the front at Ust Padenga, the company relieved retiring to the comfortable barracks at Shenkursk to relax a bit.

In the lower floor of the building we had appropriated for our quarters there lived an energetic little gray haired woman with her daughter in the late twenties, a shy, retiring, colorless female. The elder woman had been hired to tend the many stoves in the hospital buildings. She was a genius in her way. Every morning she would go from stove to stove — there must have been a half dozen at least — and in no time at all would build a fire in each. When the wood had burned down to a bed of coals the damper plate was pushed in and the coals would glow for a long time, and the heated bricks would keep the room snug and cozy until the next morning when the process was repeated. The boys called the old woman "mamma" and there developed a mutual friendliness. Around Christmas time there was the usual Yuletide conviviality, and mamma was treated to more than a few friendly libations of rum, in short she got a bit drunk, and to show her gratitude and Christmas spirit, she performed for us a couple of those national Slavic dances, clicking her heels with the utmost gusto.

There was a Y.M.C.A. building a couple of blocks to our rear which we reached by scrambling over the board fence at the limit of our back yard. There wasn't too much doing there, but there was stationery and envelopes for writing and mailing letters, and a pile of back-dated *London Times* where we could read about the St. Mihiel salient and other events that had happened three months before.[16] There was also a piano there and some of those Russian soldiers would pound out rollicking tunes and bawl out those old Muscovite ballads. Once Sir Ernest Shackleton came here.

16. One of the first offensives of World War I that involved the American Expeditionary Force, the Battle of St. Mihiel, Sept. 12-15, 1918, was fought by American and French troops led by General John J. Pershing, who drove the German army back toward the city of Metz. The American attack stalled when advancing troops outdistanced food supplies and artillery; but it demonstrated that the Americans had come to fight, and it increased their stature in the eyes of the French and British. *Doughboy Center: The Story of the American Expeditionary Forces* (http://www.worldwar1.com/dbc/stmihiel.htm).

Sometime in December a patient named Fraser, a Canadian, arrived in the hospital for a short stay. We had a few books in our library and it so happened that Fraser and I were taking turns reading Zane Grey's "Wild Fire." He was released shortly after and rejoined his company. A week or so later he was ambushed while on patrol, and his body was brought back to Shenkursk and placed temporarily in our morgue. I went in to look at him. The Bolsheviks had bashed in his skull and cut off the lower arm. This seems to have been a characteristic practice of the Reds, just as the Indians went in for scalping. They apparently carried small hatchets, comparable to the Indian's tomahawk.[17]

A week later while patrolling on horseback, another Canadian and two Yanks were ambushed by Bolos lurking in the woods. One of the Yanks escaped. The bodies were also temporarily placed in our morgue.

It was an evening sometime in December that we were aroused by a fire alarm up town. We hurried over there where quite a crowd had collected around a large, two story building burning fiercely and throwing sparks far up into the sky. Nobody was doing anything, indeed nothing could be done. I noticed our top sergeant leaning on an axe, a position he maintained throughout the evening. My buddy and I beat a surreptitious retreat to the kitchen and fixed ourselves a snack and then retired to our quarters and hit the alfalfa.

Our Freddie Beard was having his difficulties. He was a somewhat coarse and slovenly character, untidy and unkempt. Once at a stop, while going through England, and desperately craving a smoke, he had jumped out and grabbed a half smoked cigarette lying in the gutter, and smoked it, despite the razzing of his companions. During the flu epidemic at Bakaritza, Freddie, who was perturbed about catching the

17. Atrocity accounts about the behavior of troops were rife on both sides during World War I. Each side accused the other of mutilation, attacks on civilians and theft of their property, mistreatment and execution of prisoners, and rape and violence against women. For every incident that was reported and spread among the Allied troops, similar stories made the rounds among the Bolshevik forces (Antony Lockley, "Propaganda and the First Cold War in North Russia, 1918-1919: The Russian Civil War and the Propaganda Battle between the Bolshevik and British Forces on the Archangel Front," *History Today* 53 [Sept. 2003]: 46-53).

flu, was in the habit of holding a mess kit over a flame to fry the germs. Not quite the type suitable for orderly or k.p. duties, he had been assigned to the job of collecting, cleaning and replacing the many lamp chimneys in all the lamps around the buildings. He had appropriated a private cubby hole beneath a stairway for his headquarters where he ostensibly was kept busy, but in reality enjoyed considerable privacy and leisure. One day Freddie, laboring under some suppressed excitement, approached one of the k.p.'s with a proposition. During his rounds in the officer's quarters he had discovered a jug of rum. On a 50-50 basis he suggested that the k.p. come down the hall with a covered pail, and he would slip him the jug of rum, to be concealed somewhere in the horse stable. It all worked out according to plan. That night Freddie disappeared somewhere and when he returned late at night he surreptitiously slipped his accomplice a pound note. Freddie had made some clandestine connections somewhere and often at night he would disappear for parts unknown. One night he came in late, long after the lights were out and everyone had hit the sack. He was inebriated to the nth degree and started to vomit all over his bunk. McCleary who slept in the bunk next to him asserted that he pulled open the neck of his underwear and puked down the inside. He was still asleep at mid morning, and when the top sergeant came in and ordered him to "come out of your filth," Freddie whined in an aggrieved manner, "Now sergeant you let me be. I'm cold and sick."

The shortest day of the year had come. There were a few hours of gloomy daylight and then the long night descended abruptly, and the temperature dropped lower and lower, far below zero. And before we knew it the Christmas season was at hand. We had no trouble finding a Christmas tree and setting it up in the big ballroom running along the front of the second floor.

On Christmas Eve we put on a program in this room with the grand piano, the artificial palm and the decorated tree, and the patients were all assembled here. We had a singfest, some monologues and recitations. Pvt. Tomlin put on his famous cheese dance, and Eddie Kramer sang his cootie song to the tune of "Over There" — the bugs are crawling, the bugs are crawling, the bugs are crawling everywhere. Our three piece orchestra, violin, guitar, and banjo struggled through a couple of numbers. Then we were all issued Christmas stockings from the Red Cross, which included among other things a package of cigarettes, a cigar, and a can of pipe tobacco.

The cooks had outdone themselves in fixing up a special holiday dinner, and I still have a copy of the menu served.

> ### *American Field Hospital #337 Sec. B.*
> ### *Christmas Dinner Dec. 25th 1918*
>
> **Fricasee of Rabbit / Beefsteak and Onion Gravy**
> **Mashed Potatoes**
> **Mustard Pickles / Cranberry Sauce**
> **Bread / Butter**
> **Tea, Milk & Sugar**
> **Rice and Date Pudding (Peppermint Sauce)**
> **Chocolate Layer Cake**
> **Canned Peaches and Apricots**
> **Candy, Cigarettes and Dates**
>
> (Signed)
> *Perry R. Johnson*
> *Mess Sgt.*

On the day of the 25th we had planned to have a party, and our Russian nurse Marie was asked to invite a dozen or more Russian girls to attend. They did, and so did practically all the younger generation in town, including a detachment of Cossacks. It seems that parties in Russia were free-for-all affairs. We had quite a time getting rid of the undesirables, and there was not a little resentment and ill humor evinced. The schoolmaster and a flock of his bright young pupils put on a few songs for us before leaving. A balalaika orchestra was welcomed to furnish the music for the dancing a bit later.[18]

18. The balalaika musical instrument family consists of three-stringed guitar- or mandolin-like instruments with three-sided bodies, and spruce or fir tops and backs. From the highest-pitched to the lowest, they included the prima, sekunda, alto, bass, and contrabass balalaika ("The Oddmusic Gallery": http://www.oddmusic.com/gallery/index.html).

We were pleasantly surprised when we saw the girls Marie had invited. Where they had kept themselves is a mystery to me. We were too used to the peasant type barishna [woman], with the felt boots and babushka to be prepared for this. Shenkursk, it seems, was a sort of cultural center, a seat of learning, inhabited mostly by a higher, aristocratic class of people, hostile to the Bolsheviki. The girls we now saw were bright and intelligent looking, fair and lovely, some even beautiful. They were dressed in charming party dresses in the latest style, and high heeled shoes. The way they glided over the dance floor, gracefully and spiritedly in the arms of those lucky doughboys who could dance, reminded one that Russia is indeed the home of the ballet. Later on in the evening the tables were set with refreshments and we each escorted a pretty Russian damsel to a seat. The only difficulty was the language barrier, and about all we could do was to exchange smiles and such chivalrous courtesies as we could come up with, along with some desperate but futile jabbering.

IN THE DAYS FOLLOWING life again resumed its dreary course. About this time we were issued rifles and had rifle drill every day along with the usual setting up exercises. Boelens and I had contacted a washerwoman who did our clothes and underwear at a small stipend. The sauna in the back yard was kept going for the hot steam baths, and as we had acquired a horse, a detail was set to building a stall in one of the sheds at the rear. Those on night shifts were on duty from 5:30 to 7 a.m.

From the bluffs just below the town limits one could look down on the crowds of young folks skating on the river ice. It was surprising to us to see so many there as one rarely saw any in the streets.

CHAPTER FIVE

Retreat from Shenkursk

Had it not been the farthest extension of Allied line in 1919, the unknown Russian village of Ust Padenga would have remained unknown to the rest of the world. As it was, the booming Bolshevik guns that blasted away outside Ust Padenga reverberated all the way to Washington, D.C.

By December 1918, Allied leaders in Russia had settled their troops into winter quarters, expecting little action until warmer weather returned in the spring. They failed to perceive or take into account the fact that the tundra covering most of the region was much easier to navigate in winter than in summer. During the warmer months, the topsoil thaws enough for grasses and low bushes to grow; but the underlying ground remains frozen, thus holding water in swamps, marshes, and shallow ponds, confining travel to rivers and high-ground roads. With the coming of winter, the tundra freezes solid and the ice is deep enough to move troops and equipment — including heavy artillery — overland with relative ease.

Because they knew that their soldiers understood how to use the terrain and how to survive in the bitterly cold winters, Bolshevik leaders planned to fight through the winter rather than waiting for its fierce cold and long nights to pass. Aided by the darkness of the seemingly unending arctic nights, the "Bolos" — as the Allied troops called them — quietly moved their big guns and infantry troops within range of the front-line villages and began bombarding them. Once the Bolshevik heavy artillery opened fire, it did not take long for the Americans and their officers to

A heavy Bolshevik artillery bombardment, followed by a ground attack, forced the Americans to abandon Shenkursk along a little-used trail through the Russian forest. Using sleighs drawn by Russian ponies, they managed to move the wounded in their field hospital to safe quarters away from the front.
(NARS, U.S. Army Signal Corps Photograph, no. SC 152839)

realize that they held untenable positions. Heavy shells penetrated their simple wood-frame and log structures, driving out the occupants. Initially, Allied strategists thought the bombardment's purpose was to harass those closest to the front; but as it persisted and intensified, they realized they were not going to have a quiet winter.

When they were satisfied that the bombardment had sufficiently softened their opponents' fortifications, large numbers of Bolshevik fighters attacked all along the front, driving Allied troops from the small front-line villages back to larger fortifications. Those who had gotten as far as Ust Padenga made their way back to Shenkursk, but even there the shelling and ground attacks continued. The Allied command now realized that they needed to pull back further immediately, before the "Bolos" would surround them. Godfrey Anderson's hospital unit had remained at Shenkursk while the American infantrymen and a Canadian artillery unit had moved forward to Ust Padenga. Now, as soldiers from those outlying posts regrouped in Shenkursk, Bolshevik soldiers followed closely behind, making it necessary for the medics to quickly load the wounded on horse-drawn sleighs and make a night flight from Shenkursk down a back trail through the forests and frozen river valleys.

With guns booming behind them, the Allied soldiers and their wounded compatriots retreated to the Vaga River, and from there to a safe location closer to Archangel. Their retreat was successful in large part because of a group of unsung heroes: the little Russian ponies that doggedly pulled the loaded sleighs for several days with little rest. Anderson and his fellow American soldiers, many of them from Michigan farms, had been enthusiastic in their appreciation of the capabilities of these ponies since they had arrived in Russia. The stout little workers seemed to be every-

During the winter months, pony-drawn sleighs carried mail from home to soldiers stationed along the Dvina River and as far inland as Shenkursk. In the summer months mail reached soldiers in the interior by boat or railroad. (NARS, U.S. Army Signal Corps Photograph, no. SC 161099)

where, pulling sleds and wagons, hauling passengers, and serving as draft animals on the region's small farms. Standing only four to four and a half feet at the shoulder, they were hardy and hard working, as well as even-tempered, and they had thick coats that enabled them to withstand the harsh northern winters. In a 1908 book, Liberty Hyde Bailey, dean of Cornell University's College of Agriculture, wrote of the Russian ponies: "They have great endurance, and the best of them are not surpassed in usefulness by any other breed." Had they been asked, Anderson and his fellow soldiers would have promptly echoed Bailey's praise.

"There's hell at Ust Padenga!"

As I said before, the Vaga front was thrust far beyond the parallel Railroad and Dvina fronts and was exposed to flanking movements on both sides. There had been little danger during the fall months, the area between being largely swamp and morass, and all but impassible for hauling batteries across country; but now that all this terrain was frozen solid, such transportation was no longer hampered. In December the enemy hauled several batteries into position and began to bombard our farthest outpost at Ust Padenga and the two adjoining villages, some fifteen miles beyond Shenkursk. However, our own artillery managed to destroy these guns for the time being. But the ominous rumors persisted. A large invasion force, it was reported, was mobilizing at Vologda and other places. The enemy was said to be infiltrating the villages surrounding Shenkursk, especially Kodima, about thirty miles to the northeast, and was preparing to break a trail through the forest to Shenkursk. The patrols which were sent out met with various reverses: guns became immobilized by frozen oil, a mix-up of orders ended in frustrating confusion, and an elaborate Cossack patrol, which set out amid a great fanfare returned later in disorganized rout.

These baffling reverses had the effect of bolstering the confidence of the enemy, and his own patrols became bolder and more frequent. These would approach the outposts in the night and sneak up on the sentry standing numb and half frozen, his apprehension high, his morale low. They wore a sort of white tunic which rendered them all but invisible against the snowdrifts and brush extending everywhere. The whole aspect in fact had become increasingly ominous and gloomy.

We, back in Shenkursk, had little conception of the actual state of affairs up Ust Padenga way. For all we knew, everything up at the front was well under control. It was now mid January with all the rigors of the Arctic winter, and it would seem that all military activity must be suspended by the very inclemency of the weather. We did not then realize that the Russians do their best fighting in the winter. Witness Poltava, Napoleon at Moscow, Stalingrad.[1]

1. Anderson's Swedish heritage and his interest in the country's history made him

From time to time a number of our patients were from our Russian allies who were enlisted to fight the Bolsheviks. Some of these were disgustingly untidy. We had sterilized all the indoor closets and had them spotlessly clean. Instead of using the seats as all civilized people do, there were among them some oafs who squatted over the seats and deposited their excretions on the seats. Even more disgusting was their filthy habit of using their fingers instead of the toilet paper provided, and wiping them off on the newly painted walls and door frames.

Among the younger of these recruits there were a number of venereals, who seemed to look upon their malady as a huge joke.

One older patient — the schoolmaster, I believe it was — down with some terminal lung ailment, flu or consumption, had a tin can by his bedside, as did all such patients, in which they could expectorate. He was a gentle, sensitive, lovable sort of person. On one occasion he inadvertently tipped the contents of his can on the blanket. The poor fellow looked with horror on the greenish, revolting corruption and burst into hopeless tears.

The years have passed and memories fade with fleeting time, but some events are so deeply graven on the mind that they can never be forgotten. Such are the memories of that fateful nineteenth of January and the events that crowded upon each other in such rapid succession in

---

aware of the Battle of Poltava (Ukraine), where, in June 1709, Czar Peter I drove Charles XII and his Swedish army, weakened by a Russian winter, from the field, marking the end of Sweden as a European military power. Slightly more than a century later, Napoleon entered Russia with an army estimated at 400,000 to 500,000 (possibly as many as 600,000) and fought his way to Moscow, which his army seized in September 1812, after most of its occupants had fled. However, he had outdistanced his supply lines, and devastating fires had destroyed most of Moscow and the supplies he hoped to find there, forcing him to withdraw in mid-October. Attacked and harassed as they pulled back, having no supplies, and ravaged by the harsh Russian winter storms, Napoleon's forces had by spring shrunken to a bony skeleton of its initial might. Figures on how many men Napoleon took to Russia and how many eventually came back vary rather widely. But most historians agree that only about 10 percent of his total active army returned from the Russia campaign. See, e.g., Georges Lefebvre, *Napoleon from Tilsit to Waterloo* (New York: Columbia University Press, 1969), 2: 311-12; see also Eugene Tarle, *Napoleon's Invasion of Russia, 1812* (New York: Oxford University Press, 1942), p. 397, and Richard K. Riehn, *1812: Napoleon's Russian Campaign* (New York: John Wiley, 1991), pp. 77, 501.

the days that followed. It was in the darkness that preceded the dawn when we were awakened by that first sullen boom from up Ust Padenga way. It sent the echoes rattling about town and reverberating across the flats beyond the river. We lay in our bunks, alert and straining our ears to listen. Again came that sustained roll, like distant thunder. What the —— ! What's going on up there, anyway? Again and again the thunder continued. The night man, clattering up the stairs, carrying a lantern, burst into the room to wake us up for breakfast (the reveille bugle had long been discarded). "There's hell at Ust Padenga!" he said.

The bunks creaked as the men came out of the blankets. All slept in their woolen underwear, some not even removing their heavy woolen socks. Freddie Beard didn't even bother to remove his o.d. uniform and overseas cap before rolling in. Those in the upper bunks hurriedly leaned over to grab their clothes hanging on nails high on the walls near their bunks. There was the clump of feet hitting the floor. We dressed in haste, mostly in silence. For once the chronic cussing of the army was forgotten. Presently the sound of human hoofs thumping around the jog in the old stairway was heard as they departed in groups of two's and three's for the mess hall, while the sluggards and clumsy fingered strained at wrapped leggings, shoe laces, tucking in shirt tails and leather jerkins. How vividly memory recalls all this.

Outside was that blackest of darkness that precedes the dawn. The snow lay deep over all, burdening the spruces and blanketing the rooftops. The bitterness of the air was breath taking; the frost creaked beneath the hob nailed boots headed down the path to the mess hall. From off to the south an intermittent glow wavered along the horizon, like heat lightning on a summer night, throwing a dull glow over all; the bellowing of the guns came more clearly over the frosty air.

It was a day of suspense and foreboding. Daylight broke cold and clear along towards the middle of the forenoon. Smoke rose in vertical plumes from the many chimneys about town until dissipated at great heights above, undisturbed by the slightest breath of air. Throughout the day the cannonading continued but finally subsided as darkness fell. Silence brooded once more over the great tundra to the south. What in the world had happened? Had Ust Padenga fallen? No one knew! Came the evening mess: Fried bully beef. Who knew or cared! Then the anxiety and restless inactivity of the long evening.

One recalls wandering over to the Y.M.C.A. One could imagine something sinister lurking in the dark recesses among the closely packed conifers. How coldly the stars glittered in the black canopy above. How fitfully the Aurora writhed in the northern heavens. Scrambling over the fence, one soon came to the rambling monstrosity, half log and half board, that housed the Y.M.C.A. But this night the place was largely deserted. One wandered about beneath the dim glow of the oil lamps and re-read a few headlines in the ancient tattered newspapers, tried to decipher the big map of Europe on the wall printed in Cyrillic letters, until, overwhelmed by a sense of desolation, one hurried back along the deserted streets to the comparative conviviality of the barracks and climbed into one's bunk and smoked cigarette after cigarette and re-read letters from home.

Next morning the thundering began again, and continued more or less sporadically throughout the day. During the afternoon a couple of sleighs arrived from the front with the first contingent of wounded. They lay in sleeping bags on straw. Their faces were drawn and grim and they had little to say, but we learned that the long rumored enemy offensive had actually begun.

At one time that afternoon a lone sleigh pulled up at the rear of the hospital carrying a single patient, a Russian recruit. Just then my partner and I came by carrying water, being on k.p. that day. That was a miserable, back-breaking job. The water had to be carried nearly one hundred yards from the well up front and then up a flight of stairs to the kitchen, and it took many trips to supply the demand for water. At the well the bucket was drawn up by means of a windlass. The water had spilled around the well forming a sort of icy pyramid making it all but inaccessible. We came to the rear just as the ambulance sleigh did, and no one else being available we were commandeered to carry the poor fellow on a stretcher to a small room at the rear and lift him onto a cot. Being inexperienced we wrestled and heaved the patient rather clumsily, amid the angry criticism of the lieutenant in charge (Danzinger). We finally got the squealing Russkie on a cot. There was a small insignificant looking hole right in the middle of the paunch, but a nasty and perhaps mortal wound nevertheless.

There was a young driver from the Ambulance Co. who brought his sleigh of wounded to Shenkursk, but did not go back, on the grounds that his orders did not specify that he *go back*. One remembers the silent contempt with which the other ambulance company drivers regarded him as they came in daily and went back — without specific orders to do so.

About the middle of the week Corporal Thornton, with Art Larson and Frank Gurinsky, were detailed to go up to the front with medical supplies and to evacuate some wounded. They drove up by sleigh with one Pvt. Carl G. Berger from the Supply Co. The artillery was in action just beyond the far outskirts of the village and there was a great clatter of machine gun and rifle fire from blockhouses and en-trenched positions to the south. Shells were dropping in the village, part of which had been demolished. The four men went into a building to warm themselves before one of those great brick plaster stoves. The Supply Co. man was seated before the stove while the others lounged about on either side of him.

At that moment a shell came tearing through the roof and struck the stove with a tremendous crash, filling the room with a thick cloud of plaster dust. The men picked themselves up, appalled at the sight of the blood with which they were sprinkled and fearful that they had sustained serious wounds. When the dust had somewhat cleared, they were horrified to see that the shell, a dud, or one that failed to explode, had neatly clipped off the head of Pvt. Berger, just before striking the stove, and his torso reclined in the chair spouting blood like a fountain. Thus admonished to haste, the three lost no time in completing their mission and heading back to Shenkursk. That night in our barracks Gurinsky and Larson soberly shook hands in mutual congratulation.

Ust Padenga

Ust Padenga was the largest of three villages clustered close together some fifteen miles south of Shenkursk, all located on the west bank of the Vaga. Nijni Gora extended farthest toward the enemy, a half mile southwest of Ust Padenga and somewhat farther from the Vaga. It lay alongside a small tributary of the Vaga, now frozen and covered with deep snow, as was the Vaga. It was situated on a slight eminence, nearly surrounded by ravines filled with deep snow. Ust Padenga and the other village, Visorka Gora, about three-quarters of a mile further north, lay along the banks of the Vaga, the latter village just north of where the stream mentioned before enters that river. The road from Ust Padenga crossed a small bridge at this point. Just to the west, this small stream emerged from the forest and curved 90 degrees to the north, then swung in a wide semicircle to the east just before passing Visorka Gora.

A company of Cossacks occupied Ust Padenga. They had refused to occupy Nijni Gora, considering it too hazardous and difficult to withdraw from in case of emergency and so its defense was taken over by a platoon from Company A, consisting of 46 men under Lt. Mead. Half of this platoon was located at the extreme southern edge of the village under Mead, and the other half was established at the north extremity under command of a platoon sergeant. About a mile to the north the remainder of Company A, with three field pieces, under Capt. Odjard, occupied Visorka Gora.

For some time, through glasses, they had been aware of considerable activity in the villages off in the distance, with flares and rockets at night, while, as said before, the patrols were getting bolder and more frequent.

And then, before dawn on the 19th, the storm broke. Suddenly, without warning, the enemy's long silent guns opened a tremendous bombardment. These were concealed in the woods beyond the Vaga and far outranged our few 3-inch field pieces supporting Company A.[2] By the indistinct light of early dawn, Lieut. Mead swept the distant vista with his field glass. From the forest beyond the river a mile or so away, a long skirmish line of the enemy had emerged, hundreds of them, and were plowing their way, under cover of the furious barrage, through the three-foot blanket of snow that lay over all. They were as yet out of range of rifle or machine gun fire. The heavy shelling continued for about an hour unabated, then just as the approaching troops

2. Both sides were equipped with rifled artillery field pieces. The Canadian artillerymen had "18-pounders," which were supplied by the British government. The Bolsheviks had 76 mm and 122 mm guns. The 18-pounders fired a 3.3-inch shell weighing 18 pounds, with a range of about five miles. The Bolshevik 76 mm guns, which could fire at a higher trajectory, sent their 3-inch, 15-pound shells as far as eight miles. Allied forces in northern Russia had nothing to match the Bolsheviks' 122 mm guns, which could launch their 30-pound, 4.9-inch guns upwards of twelve miles.

Some native Russians fought under British officers in 1918 and 1919. This machine-gun group is being instructed by a British training officer (visible on the right).   (NARS, Still Picture Collection, no. 89944)

were coming within range, suddenly subsided. This apparently was a signal, for immediately the ravine just below was swarming with Bolsheviks in white smocks who charged up the hill with fixed bayonets and automatic weapons. These, more than a hundred, had stealthily moved up during the night and burrowed into the snow drifts, where they lay concealed until the jump off signal was given.

The startled Americans rushed to the defense as best they could, pouring a devastating fire into the onrushing ranks, their machine guns slowing down group after group, but there were too many, and others came pressing forward, firing as they came with automatic rifles, showering our thin defenses with a storm of bullets. A Cossack platoon from Ust Padenga now put in an appearance and had barely joined the defense line when, catching a full view of the hopeless odds stacked against them, immediately panicked and beat a hasty retreat, abandoning many of their arms.

Some of our men had been killed fighting desperately, others wounded. The enemy was about to overwhelm the rest with fixed bayonets and had already entered the upper village. A hasty retreat was ordered to the lower position at the other end of the town. As they started to move down the main street, a well-packed roadway, they soon became aware that the Bolos had set up a machine gun at the upper end and were in a position to enfilade the entire street. It was therefore necessary to dodge along behind the buildings lined along the street, which meant struggling through three or four feet of unbroken snow drifts, fighting from houses, sheds and outhouses, dashing as best they could across the open spaces between. Some went down, disappearing in the deep snow, never to be seen again. Somehow Lt. Mead and the survivors, each on his own, reached the second platoon at the lower village, which was desperately striving to hold off the approaching enemy.

Now that the two platoons were united under charge of their commander, the decision was to attempt an immediate retreat back to Visorka Gora to join the main unit of Company A. The prospect was appalling. There was no cover between the two points, a good half mile, and to reach the traversed road they must go down a hill drifted shoulder deep and cross an open, exposed valley. The expected artillery supposed to cover their retreat did not materialize and they could delay no longer. They had no alternative but to plunge down the hill and through the plain below, wallowing and floundering in waist deep snow, without any cover, and under vicious enemy fire. Every now and then someone was hit — killed or wounded. Some of those [hit but] not killed soon froze to death in the terrible cold. All that day the temperature had hovered near 45 degrees below zero.

The artillery support had failed because the Russian [Cossack] gunners who had relieved the Canadians, observing the horde of Bolshevik troops crossing the river and deploying from the woods and the devastation at Nijni Gora, had abandoned their guns in a panic. Capt. Odjard came up in a rage and forced them back to their battery at pistol point, but by that time it was too late to cover the retreat of Lt. Mead's platoon.

The Lieutenant and the remnants of his platoon finally stumbled through the outposts at Visorka Gora and flopped in the nearest shelter more dead than alive. Of Lt. Mead's original 46 men he now counted but seven unwounded men including himself. Lt. Hugh McPhail went out with a group of volunteers and a sleigh and brought in some of the wounded under fire. But there were seventeen never heard from again.

During the night of the 19th and 20th a group of Canadian artillerymen under Lt. Winslow pulled in from Shenkursk with two guns. At the same time the Cossack garrison at Ust Padenga, having no desire to undergo what had befallen Nijni Gora, abandoned that village so covertly under darkness that the enemy was unaware that the village was deserted.

Now for the rest of the day and most of the night the enemy turned his guns on our positions at Visorka Gora. The five block-houses, however, stood the pounding well and there were few casualties throughout the rest of the village. For the next two days — the 20th and the 21st — repeated waves of the enemy attempted to storm our positions, but were repulsed with a frightful slaughter, the Canadian gunners especially wreaking havoc among the massed troops. Still believing that Ust Padenga was occupied, the Bolos subjected the village to a tremendous pounding by their artillery, then sent waves of infantry to the attack over the same open snow fields over which our own troops had made their disastrous retreat a couple of days before. They advanced in the face of a vigorous artillery, machine gun, and rifle fire which transformed the valley into a bloody shambles and by the time they had "captured" the deserted village, the whole area was littered with hundreds of dead and dying lying in the snow.

It was about this time that the enemy decided to change his offensive tactics. Finally realizing that they could not over-run our position by direct infantry assault, they redoubled the artillery bombardment. Shells came over by the thousands but we could not respond, being outranged. Our little force was growing smaller day by day through attrition. Casualties were increasing. A heavily timbered building had been set up for a hospital in the most protected location in the village. Lt. Ralph Powers, the lone medical officer attached to Co. A, had been working for three days and nights with little or no sleep. He was operating on a wounded soldier just brought in, beneath the dim light of an oil lamp. Several others were present, warming themselves by the stove, and listening to the rattling of gunfire and the thunder of Soviet artillery. At that moment a shell crashed through the roof and exploded as it hit the wall. Three of the bystanders were killed instantly; the wounded soldier still lay on the cot but one of his legs had been blown off and he died shortly after. Lt. Powers lay on the floor, mangled and bleeding and apparently mortally wounded. Drivers from the Ambulance Co. rushed him to the hospital at Shenkursk, where he died shortly after.

The situation at Visorka Gora was rapidly deteriorating. It was learned that the battle here was part of a large enveloping movement with Shenkursk as the main objective. There was danger that Co. A would be surrounded and cut off. Orders came in to evacuate the place at 10 p.m. on the 22nd. The Reds had begun to use incendiary shells, and just as the column was about to leave one of these landed on one of the main buildings of the town which immediately erupted into flame. The wounded and transportable supplies went on ahead, while the rest of the cavalcade, heavily burdened, brought up the rear. The Canadians had trouble moving their two guns along the slippery road. Some of their horses had been killed by bursting shells, the others much weakened through exposure. One of the two guns skidded and tipped over into a ditch and the most strenuous efforts of both men and beasts failed to dislodge the eighteen-pounder. They removed the breechblock and carried it with them to Shenkursk where we are told it was thrown down a well. All through the frigid night they stumbled over the frozen ruts and potholes in the wretched road which wound through miles of virtually impenetrable forests. Far in their rear an angry red glow suffused the sky from the burning village [Visorka Gora] they had evacuated. Half frozen, dead tired and famished with hunger, they finally reached the village of Sholosha about seven in the morning of the 23rd.

It was decided to remain here and rest for the day and resume their journey at nightfall. The weary troops crowded into the various buildings along the village street, thawed out their tinned rations, then flopped on the floor to drop off into a fitful slumber. The Cossacks, on the other hand, were restless and uneasy, milling about and reluctant to halt. Also they had got hold of some rum and made a lot of noisy commotion in the street; there were all kinds of wild rumors floating around; some of the horses had got loose and were dashing about, adding to the noise and confusion. And then some inebriated idiot started to blast away with his rifle under the impression that the Reds were closing in. Most of Company A, aroused by the racket, rushed out expecting to engage in instant battle. Capt. Odjard figured the best way to terminate the excitement and confusion was to line up and continue the march to the village of Spasskoe, about four miles farther on. The men had had but little rest and the road was largely uphill and the going tough in the darkness. There were signs that enemy patrols had bypassed our troops on both sides of the Vaga as there were signal lights from church towers in both directions. The column passed through several small villages of doubtful loyalty. However, they passed through the gauntlet without incident, probably the enemy sentries mistaking our troops for their own marching columns. Our troops reached Spasskoe at four o'clock in the morning and turned into whatever shelter they could find to snatch a bit of sleep.

From the bluff at Spasskoe there was an extensive view of the plain along the river, but in the darkness before the dawn nothing could be seen except the flashing of distant signal lights. Capt. Odjard sent out a mounted Cossack patrol to reconnoiter the enemy movements. They returned about seven o'clock, gloomy and pessimistic, reporting that thousands of enemy troops were marching towards Shenkursk. Somewhat skeptical, Capt. Moffat (of the Canadian Field Artillery) and Lt. Mead climbed up into the church tower at the first light of dawn and surveyed the area through their field glasses. One glance confirmed the Cossacks' report. Long lines of artillery and infantry were moving along the roads converging on the town, and in the plain below massed troops were moving up for the attack. Already the first shells were landing near the village. Capt. Odjard immediately roused his troops and set up a skirmish line at the edge of the bluff. A bit to the right stood the village church surrounded by the churchyard with tombstones protruding from the snow. Across the road were some extensive woodpiles near which Capt. Moffat set up his gun position, whose fire he directed from the church tower, which he used as an observation post. A telephone wire had been strung along the trees to establish communication with Shenkursk, some four miles to the north.

The physical condition of Co. A was poor and the morale low.

They were groggy from loss of sleep and weak from inadequate food and near the limit of their endurance. This rendered them unusually sensitive to the cold, although the temperature that day was comparatively warm, having risen to zero. For that reason small groups were permitted in turn to enter a building close by and warm themselves by the stove for five minutes while awaiting the attack.

However, the Soviets, from recent experience, had no stomach for further exposure to the deadly Canadian artillery. They chose to make use of their own superior artillery to dislodge the Americans from their position in Spasskoe without exposing their infantry to wholesale slaughter. They therefore cut loose with a terrific bombardment, and the shells began bursting all over the village, splintering log buildings, ripping up the street, scattering tombstones, woodpiles and snow in all directions, one piece of shrapnel even clanging against the church bell. Later in the day the brave Capt. Moffat, while unconcernedly strolling over to his gun, was severely wounded by an exploding shell. He was rushed in a sleigh to the Shenkursk hospital, where he died shortly after.

A bit later, about 1:30 p.m., a shell landed directly on the lone Canadian field gun, wrecking it and killing one of the gunners. Capt. Odjard, who was standing in the vicinity, was wounded severely in the neck and in turn was transported to Shenkursk.

The situation now was hopeless. The bombardment was increasing in intensity, our last piece of artillery was gone, which the enemy would certainly soon realize; and then he could launch an overwhelming infantry assault against the depleted and exhausted defenders. A call was made to Shenkursk asking for orders but before any could come a shell severed the wire and cut off connections, so Lt. Mead wisely took it upon himself to order a retreat to that place.

The company arrived at Shenkursk about four o'clock in the afternoon of January 24th. They had not had time for dinner at Spasskoe but the cooks were unwilling to discard the cans of hot stew they had prepared, but sent it along in the convoy insulated as best they could. The famished troops now went for this almost in a frenzy, even digging it out with their hands. Others went after the rum jugs to help obliterate their recollections. In any event the entire outfit had then flopped in whatever place was available and immediately dropped off into the profound slumber of utter exhaustion.

Shenkursk Again

And now the afternoon was drawing to a close. It had been a hectic day. Most of the convalescing patients and those with minor ailments had been conveyed to an upper dormitory in Hospital No. 2, and I for one had been assigned to duty in those quarters. Some of the Russian civilians had got wind of developments and were restless and apprehensive. There was a middle-aged Russian woman who had been hired for duties in the kitchen below hospital No. 2. Once when I came through there she seized me in a terrified grip and started an incoherent and hysterical jabbering. I went over to the main hospital on an errand and ran across Freddie Beard at the hole in the fence where a couple of boards had been knocked out to make a passageway. As we were exchanging a few remarks, a young Limey orderly came hurrying by, all excited. He paused to inform us that the town was surrounded and that none of us would get out alive. Freddie turned on him in disgust and spat out the expletive, "Oh s — t!" However, as events proved, the situation was indeed rather more critical than we suspected at the time.

I found the main hospital a bedlam of confusion. People were rushing about the corridors, clattering up and down the great central stairway, everyone busy and in a hurry.

I looked in at the large reception room at the rear of the west wing. There were a number of casualties there, some lying on stretchers still awaiting attention. Others sat about on the floor unwinding the first-aid dressings about the leg or arm. Some sat propped against the wall smoking cigarettes. The floor was strewn with garments and bloody rags. Some of the medics and Russian nurses were struggling as best they could, undermanned as they were. In another room the medical officers were working desperately in surgery.

There were more than ninety patients already lying in various wards around the place. The largest was the one in front on the second floor. Just four weeks before it had served as a ballroom, brightly lighted, with a Christmas tree, and where pretty barishnas had danced with American doughboys to the strains of a balalaika orchestra. There was little activity here now, no sounds but of labored breathing, some unconscious and near death. Some were even now rigid in death, but until the living could be cared for, none could be spared to carry them out to the morgue. Among those lying here dead was the brave Lt. Powers and that gallant Canadian, Capt. Moffat.

I hurried back to hospital No. 2 and climbed the stairway at the rear to the second-floor ward facing the street. Chancing to glance through one of the windows facing the large open space where the Cossack cavalry used to drill, I noticed a bustling activity over by the stables. Presently the [stables] burst into flames and being filled above with hay began to burn furiously. I wondered about that but did not sense any imminent significance at the time.

The gloom of the early Arctic twilight was beginning to merge with the shadows beneath the encircling pines. The sky was overcast but to the north the Aurora had begun its agonized writhing. A fine, stinging snow was in the air. The cold was increasing; it would be far below zero before morning.

The firing had ceased. The enemy had dropped a few experimental shells about the town, and having established the range, was now waiting for morning to begin the bombardment. From the cathedral with the five inverted onion-shaped domes came the doleful clang of the vesper bells, but no sound came from the great monastery at the other outskirts of the town. It lay cold, bleak and silent behind its high white walls. Suddenly night had fallen!

Later that evening we were given orders to prepare all the patients, now a hundred more or less, for evacuation to the base hospital down the river. What it was all about we did not realize at the time, and no one bothered to tell us. We received further orders to hang blankets over the windows, lest those trigger happy Bolos be tempted to fire a salvo at the lighted building. It was no easy task to tuck some of those wounded patients into sleeping bags. Some of them were so badly injured that the slightest touch would cause excruciating agony, but there was need for urgent haste and we had no alternative but to stuff the patient in the bag as best we could despite his agonized screams. Then there were those shell shock cases, who raved and struggled and fought, and finally had to be overpowered by brute force.

The patients were tucked in the straw, in pairs, in the bottom of each sleigh, covered with blankets and then checked by the medical officers, given a shot of medication or a swig of rum, as the case might be. We could but wonder where they had managed to commandeer all those sleighs and ponies. They were filled up as soon as they moved into place, and then moved on to halt in a long line to await the order to move out. Those lying dead in the room upstairs were to be left behind. The British High Command had suggested that the wounded, and other patients also, be left behind, but this the American officers flatly refused to consider. So did the Canadians when it was recommended that they leave their guns behind, and they were accordingly established in a position near the head of the column.

We of the 337th F. H., having loaded the last of the patients, were sent over to the barracks building with orders to put on the Shackleton boots, which we had never used before, put on the ankle length overcoats over our sweaters, o.d. uniforms and leather jerkins, plus mufflers, double mittens, and fur caps, in addition to rifle, bayonet and ammunition. Personally I did not realize that we were leaving Shenkursk for good, and for that reason left some of my personal belongings, letters and the like, behind. We also left behind our tin helmets, gas masks and barracks bags.

Upon rejoining the convoy and looking over the crowded streets, the excitement and the chaotic confusion, it became apparent that we were actually leaving Shenkursk, probably forever. Over at British headquarters, during the afternoon, the military situation had been evaluated. The enemy had already moved up their heavy artillery, 9-inch and 7-inch guns, besides several howitzers; a number of craters about town attested to this. The lone communication wires had been cut. The earlier gun flashes indicated that the town was largely encircled, even to the northeast and northwest through which any withdrawal or retreat must pass. There was evidence also that enemy troops were stationed somewhere along the main evacuation road leading north. The alternatives then were to attempt a desperate fighting withdrawal, or to stay and attempt to survive a devastating bombardment, with no hope of relief possible from across the all but impassable ice and snow bound vastness. The result was a decision to evacuate and that immediately.

The dead tired, utterly exhausted members of Co. A were roused from their brief slumbers and informed of the new orders. Amid plaintive protests, intermingled with rage and bitter curses when they recalled the sufferings and sacrifices they had made to hold this important position, they collected their gear and stumbled out into the street. Co. C came out in better condition, but not too happy at the turn of events. Many a prized possession was thrown away to make room for the essentials. The great stores of equipment, clothing and rations were thrown out in heaps, and each soldier was free to take what he pleased, but being admonished not to overburden themselves and thus hamper their chances of getting through. What was abandoned was immediately appropriated by those civilians, who, of necessity, had to remain behind. Came midnight, when the cavalcade was scheduled to move out; but it was nowhere near ready. The dimly lighted streets of Shenkursk were crowded with confused and frightened people, milling about or scurrying hither and yon in all directions. Many civilians, who had good reason to fear the invading enemy, had procured sleighs and loaded these to capacity with what of their prized possessions they could pile on, with the smallest of youngsters perched on top. They were desperately trying to disentangle themselves from the confused assembly of neighboring rigs and get in line somewhere. Among these refugees we noticed a number of those comely young barishnas who had danced so gaily at our Christmas ball so short a time before. Irascible staff officers were riding about, issuing instructions and trying to establish some sort of order.

It was sometime after one o'clock when the convoy got the go ahead signal. Because of a report that a couple hundred of the enemy were posted astride the main road, it had been decided, as a sort of desperate gamble, to leave town by way of a little-used backwoods road which disappeared into the woods to the north and rejoined the main road some twelve miles beyond. The mounted Cossack scouts had reconnoitered this unbroken trail for some distance and reported no enemy obstruction ahead; [the latter] no doubt considering this primitive trail hopelessly snow bound and impassible.

The Cossacks were now in the lead, already buried somewhere in the gloom of the forest, followed by the Canadian artillery. Now at last the hospital convoy got under way, more than fifty sleighs with over a hundred (now) sick and wounded. When the last of these had passed along the monastery wall, the foot soldiers, British, American and Russian, numbering about a thousand, who were halted on Vologda St., now fell into line and passed through the maze of barbed wire entanglements strung about the town. They passed the last of the outlying blockhouses at the edge of town.

The civilian refugees, about 5,000, brought up the rear. Jittery and terrified, they struggled to get their topheavy sleighs into line. All were plodding along beside their rigs, men, women and children alike, except for the tots, who were bundled atop the sleigh, staring wide-eyed and frightened. Sometimes a rig would get stuck in the drifts and the whole family had to get behind and push. Sometimes a rig would tip over and strew the contents of the sleigh around in the drifts and the driver would throw up his hands wailing and imploring assistance from one or all of the Byzantine saints. The plight of these good people could not but evoke our sympathy, despite our concern with our own troubles. They were fleeing from an implacable and vindictive foe, abandoning their homes and most of their belongings to hopefully seek some friendly sanctuary far to the north.

Shenkursk to Shegovari

We of the 337th F.H. found ourselves struggling along with our convoy in almost total darkness. The huge spruces crowding the trail, their branches bending with the weight of the snow, loomed overhead, shutting off most of any feeble light that might have filtered through. On each side of the passage the snow lay in a blanket three or four feet deep. The many sleighs that had gone through had formed a couple of deep slippery ruts, while the space between was pock-marked by a continuous series of pits where the horses had trod. It was impossible to see these in the dark and every few steps a man would stumble and fall, and with difficulty get to his feet, weighted down as he was with heavy equipment.

The ordeal was especially tough for those men of Co. A bringing up the rear. They had been active for nearly a week, with little sleep. They had started out in double file but could not keep that formation, eventually straggling along as best they could, some falling asleep as they stumbled along, falling down again and again, unable and even unwilling to rise and having to be helped and urged to continue. Soon all excess baggage was thrown to the side, in a desperate effort to survive that terrible march. One platoon had cut off a couple of feet from the bottom of those ankle length overcoats, which proved to be a practical expedient. Later on more equipment would be abandoned, packs, bayonets and some even heaved the heavy overcoats, finding them too heavy and cumbersome.

As for myself struggling blindly along slipping and skidding in those unbroken-in Shackleton boots which, though indeed warm, had shiny leather soles, with no traction whatever. Time and time again I found myself taking nosedives and sprawling in the ruts because of the impossible footing. One had to scramble up in a hurry as well as he could lest he be trampled on by the horse he knew was following close behind. Although it was around 35 degrees below zero and an icy draught swept through the passageway, I had soon worked up a sweat. Nevertheless the muffler covering my mouth and nostrils soon clogged with icicles, which had to be cleared away to permit breathing. During all that agonizing peregrination, unaware of where any of my company were, I did not once sneak a ride on the sleigh I followed. However, whenever the terrain sloped downhill I got a bit of relief by stepping on the runners. I had developed a respect and consideration for those tough little Russian ponies and felt ashamed to add to their burden (although some did). After what seemed an interminable time the trail began to slope downward sharply and presently the cavalcade emerged from the confinement of the forest into the open expanse of the frozen Vaga. Here visibility improved slightly so that one could see dimly a few yards ahead and behind, but after crossing on the ice the ragged column plunged again into the Stygian gloom.[3]

Toward morning, just as a gray light began to appear in the far southeast, the guns began to open up on Shenkursk, now some ten or twelve miles to our rear. Evidently the enemy was not yet aware that the birds had flown the coop. Nevertheless, the sullen booming caused a momentary acceleration of the pace for a few minutes but it soon relapsed into the same monotonous grind.

About an hour later, when a gloomy daylight had arrived at last, the column was halted alongside a stretched-out straggling village called Yemska Gora, lying where the woods had been thinned some-

---

3. Stygian is related to the River Styx, in Greek mythology a river that formed the boundary between earth and the underworld (Hades), thus gloomy and hellish.

what. Most of the troops swarmed into the houses along the wayside to thaw out, and get a drink of water, their canteens being frozen solid; and where they sought to get a swig of hot tea from the ubiquitous samovar. Here they attempted to thaw out their cans of corned beef and slumgullion and munch their frozen hardtack.[4] Some of the Russian refugees took advantage of the delay to crowd past and get better positions farther away from the precarious rear.

After a half hour or more the grinding march was resumed. However, in the light of day it was easier to pick our way and avoid the worst potholes. The wind had subsided; the weather turned calm but remained frigid and later on became relatively brighter. Hour by hour passed; the wretched trail seemed interminable. The straggling column had stretched out a half mile beyond its original length. Later in the afternoon we passed a number of large wooden windmills — the Don Quixote type. A bit later we crossed some open country where the trail ascended a long incline to an elevation where one had a good view of the surrounding country and the winding column stretching to the front and rear as far as the eye could reach.

It was late afternoon, approaching dusk, when we finally reached Shegovari. This village is over twenty miles straight north of Shenkursk as the crow flies, but of course much longer when following the circuitous trails we had followed. Shegovari lies on the Vaga, which continues on to the north some four miles or so then reverses itself in a tremendous loop and returns to a point about a mile cross from Shegovari, where it again turns to the north and after a series of erratic convolutions passes Kitsa, some fifteen miles in a straight line due north of Shegovari.

This village was garrisoned by a few troops from Companies C and D. These had been harassed by enemy marauding parties, disguised as peasants, who on one occasion had butchered one sentry with axes and carried off another. Just the day before, some 200 of the enemy had surreptitiously stolen into the town unobserved, but prompt and violent action had forced them to retire.

We of the 337th immediately unloaded the wounded and carried

4. "Slumgullion" was a slang term for a watery, unappetizing meat and vegetable stew.

them into what seemed to be a barn and barracks combined. All had survived the ordeal except the schoolmaster mentioned before. He had quietly died unobserved somewhere along the trail. The survivors were fed and cared for as best we could and were stowed away somewhere for the night. We ourselves had been on the go for 36 hours and had traveled nearly 30 miles on foot over the toughest kind of going and were more than ready to hit the alfalfa. And that, in effect, is just what we did. Some of us flopped down in a hay loft in the barn just mentioned, not bothering to remove any clothing, not even the ponderous overcoat, Shackleton boots and fur cap. What went on around town during the night, we never knew, as we slept late the following morning. After breakfasting on bully beef, hot tea and hardtack, and ministering to our patients, we lounged about during the rest of the short remaining daylight.[5] Many of various units were milling about in the open-faced, snow-covered area below the barn loft. Three or four steps led up to an entrance to the main building. I remember an officer mounting those slippery steps, skidd[ing] and [taking] an undignified tumble to the ground below. During the afternoon some of the men had somehow obtained nails and leather and were busy nailing cleats on their Shackleton boots.

The short day had passed all too quickly and just before the lowering gloom of late afternoon the sleighs were brought in line again and the patients were carried out in their sleeping bags and tucked in the straw as before. There was a continuous clatter of machine guns at the edge of the town somewhere. Shegovari lies high on a bluff overhanging the Vaga and the trail descends a steep incline before reaching the river. To keep the sleighs from skidding sideways and overturning, a detail of medics was called and two were stationed at opposite sides of each sleigh, and [they] threw themselves lengthwise in the snow while grasping the sides to check any sideways swerving off the course during the descent. As soon as one pair of escorts reached the level of the river, they reclimbed up that arduous slope to guide in turn another sleigh down. All that took some time and it was dark when our company finally packed up its gear and hit the trail. The infantry fell in

---

5. "Bully beef" is soldier slang for boiled canned corned beef, from the French *bouilli* ("boiled").

later, followed by the refugees, with the Cossack cavalry bringing up the rear. The Vaga stretched off in a wide snowbound expanse in both directions.

Shegovari to Kitsa

Beyond the river we plunged into the forest again. Those awesome, majestic forests! One writer has described them this way:

> An unutterable stillness, an infinite fairyland of enchanted wonders. Invisible hands of artistry had draped the countless pines with garlands and wreaths of white with filmy aigrettes and huge ponderous globes and festoons woven by the frost in an exquisite and fantastic handiwork and when the sun came out as it did for a few moments, every ornament on those decorated Christmas trees glittered and twinkled with the magic of 10,000 candles. It was an enchanted toyland spread before us and we were spellbound by a profusion of airy wonders that unfolded without end as we threaded our way through a forest flanked by the straight towering trunks.[6]

But traveling in the nighttime as we did, that forest became a gloomy, sinister, ominous wilderness, fraught with hidden menace. The hospital convoy was far ahead and this time we could manage to grab a ride now and then. At rare intervals we passed along treeless openings (it might have been the Vaga), and looking back from one of these, a bit later, we could see the angry red glow in the sky far to the rear. The Cossacks had fired Shegovari and all the supplies we were forced to abandon. That eerie stretch from Shegovari to Kitsa seemed devoid of villages or even a single dwelling, at least not seen in the darkness, until we reached Vistafka, some four miles from Kitsa, the latter being about twenty miles from Shegovari. This was as far as the Vaga column had planned to retreat, and exhausted as they were, they made ready to defend this position, which, however, left much to be desired. It stood on a high bluff on the right bank of the river, which

6. Joel R. Moore, Harry H. Mead, and Lewis E. Jahns, *The History of the American Expedition Fighting the Bolsheviki* (Detroit, 1920), p. 105.

wound around the bluff in another of its serpentine loops. The area about was thickly forested and there were several other unimportant villages in the vicinity.

The infantry halted here and most of them dropped to the ground from sheer exhaustion. The refugees, however, coming up from behind with their overloaded sleighs, seized the opportunity to forge ahead, passing the halted troops by floundering through the deep snow at each side of the trail.

Immediately and in the days following they set up defenses — barbed wire, and, the ground being frozen too solid to dig into, snow trenches were laid out. (For the record, the enemy was unable to dislodge the defenders after two months of violent bombardment, which practically razed the village, and there were numerous violent assaults which were repeatedly repulsed.)

The rest of the convoy proceeded on to Kitsa, which they reached somewhere around midnight. Kitsa also lies on the Vaga, and across the river is another town called Ignatenskaya, yclept Ignatz by the doughboys. As I remember it, the convoy transporting most of the wounded and sick continued on to Beresnik, while some of the 337th remained at Kitsa. For my part I was given the assignment of guarding the horses in a large open-faced shelter constructed for them. I was relieved in an hour and went upstairs in a large ramshackle building and flopped beside some of my comrades bedded down on the floor. When I say "bedded," I mean they were simply lying in their overcoats and fur caps just as when they were traveling. The Captain came around and gave each of us a stiff shot of rum. Nevertheless we slept soundly and were roused rather late in the morning. Some of us were detailed to unload an ambulance sleigh that had just arrived from the front. The weather was extremely cold and the air was like a frosty white fog. The ambulance driver was gloomy and pessimistic and informed us that we would never get out alive as the enemy was advancing in overwhelming numbers.

My partner and I went to the sleigh. Two wounded men were lying on the straw in the bottom. The first of the wounded was pulled out by a couple of bearers and we started to pull out the second one. He lay in a grotesque posture, his legs appearing strangely contorted. As we were moving the stretcher, the soldier began to mumble in a thick and all but incoherent garble, "Quit pulling my hair." Taking a closer look, we noticed he had been creased by a bullet along the left side of the skull, and the brains had oozed out and were frozen in the straw, and in moving him we were actually pulling out his brains.

We carried the two casualties into the dark kitchen. The first one was set on a table, and his clothing removed above the waist. He had been hit twice by bullets from a swinging machine gun, which had hit him on both sides of the chest. In front were two small insignificant holes, but in the back the dumdum bullets had torn out two ragged holes, each large enough to insert a doubled fist. The medical officer (Kinyon) stuffed the holes with greased gauze. By the way, the officer stood in his leather jerkin and fur cap, while the writer had the honor to hold a lamp to give what illumination could be had. The patient was conscious during the dressing of his wound, and as we later set him up against the wall, we asked him if it hurt much. "If it don't nothing ever did," was the way he put it. The other patient, nicknamed "Doughnuts" because his name sounded something like that, was likewise set on the table and held upright, while the medical officer took a pair of scissors and proceeded to trim the protruding brains even with the skull, then filling the cavity with gauze. He also was conscious but in a mental stupor.

That afternoon, now clear and quite bright, Micky Mead and I were delegated to ride over to Vistafka on some mission. We retraced that rugged trail about as fast as the pony could go. Vistafka that day was quiet and there was no sign of the enemy, although there was an air of sullen brooding and something sinister about the area, there being a number of snipers concealed in the woods across the valley, who now and then picked off one of our men. We completed our mission without delay and lost no time in beating it back to Kitsa.

Kitsa to Beresnik

The short afternoon quickly waned, and twilight and darkness came on with characteristic suddenness. With darkness a few of us drew another assignment. A number of new casualties (including Doughnuts and his companion) had arrived during the day, and it was decided to convey them to the hospital at Beresnik during the night to avoid being waylaid by any lurking band of the enemy who might be in the area. We crossed the Vaga for the nth time and plunged again into the forest primeval, as it were. We followed more or less the general course of the Vaga. Here and there we passed bits of open country, hills and dales over which our little convoy of five or six sleighs passed, we walking beside them. The night was comparatively light although I don't recall a moon — perhaps it was the flamboyance of the Aurora, which went berserk at times.

However, after several hours floundering on the trail, we came to a village called Ust Vaga, where there was a sort of way station run by a detachment of the medical corps. It was a large two-story log building facing the main road. We pulled in alongside this building and carried in all our patients through a side door (the main entrance). Here they were given hot tea and other refreshments (all except Doughnuts, who was in a coma). Ust Vaga lies near the confluence of the Vaga and Dvina rivers.

After a half hour's rest, the patients were carried out, each on his own stretcher, and the journey was resumed. We were a little more than halfway to Beresnik, our destination. But as said before, the visibility was fairly good, not that impenetrable darkness of the night we left Shenkursk. We, the attendants of the convoy, had walked in a group near the rear for the sake of companionship. It was sometime after midnight when our attention was diverted to a disturbance in one of the sleighs ahead. It seems that poor Doughnuts was going through a series of death struggles and his companion was upset and in need of moral support. The convoy was halted and we crowded around the sleigh and impotently watched the poor fellow breathe his last.[7] His companion, tucked in beside him, pleaded with us to remain by the side of the sleigh, as he had no inclination to ride through the night alone with a dead man.

Sometime during the night, I don't recall the exact time, we finally arrived at the 337th Field Hospital Section A, a mile to the north of Beresnik on the Dvina bluffs. [The medics there] immediately took over our grim cargo, and after we had a snack and a thawing out, found us a place to spend the night.

---

7. "Doughnuts" was Pvt. Isador Dunaetz, Co. C, 339th Infantry. He was from Sodus, Michigan, and is listed as having died on January 31, 1919.

CHAPTER SIX

Respite at Beresnik

Not until they had reached the Dvina River, and then had made their way another ten miles downstream to Beresnik, did the Americans feel safe. There, at least until the spring thaw would open the river to travel, they were able to relax for the first time since they had begun their trip upriver nearly four months earlier. During that time they had befriended many Russian villagers, and now they had good reason to worry about the fate of those noncombatants as they left them behind, vulnerable to the advancing Bolsheviks. At the same time, the Americans had also developed a grudging respect for the Bolshevik fighters. Although they often had only rudimentary training, and had a variety of uniforms and equipment, the Bolsheviks knew their terrain well, and they used that knowledge effectively.

While they had proved that they could drive the Allies from their isolated outposts, the Bolsheviks were not yet ready to engage the tighter, well-fortified perimeter around Archangel. In any case, their leaders had proved that they understood the importance of winning the public-information battle. Their offensive had achieved one of its desired effects: when news reached the United States, calls to bring the troops home quickly grew to a loud chorus.

While Godfrey Anderson and his colleagues cared for the wounded and rested at Beresnik, back in the United States the sentiment and appeals to end the Russian intervention grew louder and more insistent. Critical appraisals of the expedition's leadership and news that anti-Bolshevik Russians refused to go to the front followed reports of heavy Allied fatalities from the Bolshevik counteroffensive. British and Canadian newspapers were equally strident as they issued editorial calls for the return of their troops from Russia. They no longer supported the plan that Winston Churchill once declared was intended to "strangle at birth the Bolshevik State."

In Russia, too, the Allied troops had tired of the fight. In February 1919, two British sergeants refused to continue fighting, and members of an American unit circulated a petition calling for the removal of American troops from Russia. Although the resisters were disciplined, the message Allied leaders were hearing both from Russia and on the home front was the same: it was time to bring the soldiers home.

British military leaders still argued that they could prevail if they received reinforcements. But President Wilson, who was at the Versailles Treaty negotiations, and whose eye was on the greater prize of the creation of a League of Nations, did not want ongoing fighting in Russia to impede his negotiations. He bowed to public pressure, and, as abruptly as they had learned that they were destined for Archangel, Godfrey Anderson and his fellow Americans got the news that Wilson intended to withdraw all American troops once the ice melted and troop ships had access to the Archangel harbor.[1] Preparations for departure began in the spring of 1919, as all of the American troops gathered in Archangel to await their return trip. By early July, they were all on their way home.

British, Canadian, and French troops did not return to their home countries quite so quickly. Officers of the British command were reluctant to admit that the mission had failed; but they finally succumbed to public pressure. On July 7, 1919, eight months after the Armistice ending World War I had been announced, the order went out for all remaining Allied troops to evacuate northern Russia. A British marine battalion arrived to guard British emplacements at the ports of Archangel and Murmansk during the withdrawal. By the end of August, all of the original Allied troops who had been sent to Russa a year earlier, including the French infantry units and the Canadian artillerymen who were so instrumental in protecting the retreat from Shenkursk, were either on their way home or soon would be.

1. *Chicago Observer,* Feb. 10, 1919; *New York Times,* Feb. 8, 18; Mar. 15; Apr. 4, 5, 11; Sept. 9, 1919.

"Days of leisure and relaxation"

After that episode, I was assigned for duty at the first-aid station at Ust Vaga, some sixteen miles from the base at Beresnik to the north. It lies a short distance from the Vaga River and about ten miles from where it enters the Dvina. This way station (as mentioned before) was a large two-story log building, with a large barn attached to the rear. We had quarters in a large room on the second floor; this room extended across the entire front of the building.

The threat of Bolshevik artillery barrages caused members of the Allied Expeditionary Force to sandbag around their barracks, even those close to Archangel. (NARS, Still Picture Collection, no. 96750-22)

Ust Vaga

I was destined to be here for some time, a few days in January and most of February. The front line at Vistafka appeared to be holding its own, despite a continuous bombardment and repeated infantry assaults. Ust Vaga was an ideal spot for the convoys of wounded traveling from the front to the Beresnik hospital, to stop for hot tea and refreshments.

These were largely days of leisure and relaxation, with not much to do. I lay in my bunk a good deal of the time reading Scott's "Peveril of the Peak."[2] Some of our group spent most of their time playing poker. Now and then a detail would go out and bring back a load of hay from some stacks in a snowbound field a half mile away. One time we put on a sort of entertainment inviting some Russian young folks and part of another military unit. There was balalaika music, songs, recitations and the like. A Yank from another outfit recited an original poem, the conclusion of each stanza ending with the lines, "For Ch —— sake get some transports in Archangel, for we're sick of hardtack, bully beef and tea." There were some cute young barishnas there, mostly blondes.

We were bothered a good deal by cooties. You could see some harassed individual sitting with his undershirt turned inside out picking out the pests. As a last resort one would hang the lice-ridden undershirts outside overnight in hopes of exterminating the little varmints, by exposure to far below zero temperature. It was at this time that I wrote a facetious article for the *American Sentinel* on the best method of exterminating cooties. I never kept a copy but it exists somewhere in the extant files of that paper.[3] Once Lieut. Danzinger came in and spent an affable evening, and for one thing taught us poker solitaire. Our stay here was indeed rather monotonous. Now and then a soldier came in requiring a prophylactic.[4]

One thing I especially remember. Late one evening an ambulance

---

2. *Peveril of the Peak* (1823) is Sir Walter Scott's novel about the English Civil War.

3. This humorous essay is included in this volume at Appendix C.

4. In medical terms, *prophylaxis* is any procedure to prevent the development or worsening of a disease; however, Anderson is using "prophylactic" to designate a condom, which was the common usage of his day.

Soldiers had to submit to mandatory delousing—which they called "cootie hunts"—when they returned from the front.   (NARS, U.S. Army Signal Corps Photograph, no. SC 159497)

rig pulled up to the side door. The drivers, on an unpleasant detail, stopped for the usual refreshments and relaxation. They said they had the body of Dr. Tukinoff outside and seemed undecided as to where to bring him. Out of curiosity I took a lantern and went outside for a look. There in the bottom of the sleigh lay the doctor, a collaborator with the Allied medical units. He was completely exposed, lying in his disarrayed suit of underwear. The enemy had bashed in the top of his head, and the stump of his arm, which they had hacked off, protruded stiffly. It was indeed a gruesome spectacle beneath the solitary light from the lantern, and the agonized flares of the Aurora in the northern sky. Someone had written a description of this spectacular phenomenon:

"The Aurora Borealis cannot be pictured by brush or pen. It has action, color, sheets of light, spires, shafts, beams and broad finger-like spreadings that come and go, filmy veins of light, winding and drifting in, weaving in and out among the beams and shifts, now glowing, now fading. It may be low in the north or spread over more than half the heavens. It may shift from east to western quarters of the northern heavens. Never twice the same, never repeating the delicate pattern, nor staying a moment for the admirer, it brightens or glimmers, advances or retreats, dies out gradually or vanishes quickly. Always a wonder to the soldier, who never found a night too cold for him to go and see, was the Aurora Borealis."

Ust Vaga to Osinova

Somewhere near the end of February, the 337th F.H. Section B was moved over to a place called Osinova. This village extends less than a mile along a street located a half mile from and parallel to the Dvina River. It lies across the river from Beresnik but is nearly a mile further upstream. The village is bisected by a stream running across the street during the spring freshets but is virtually dry at other times. At the north end of the street is the ornate cathedral, its bell continually proclaiming the numerous holidays and holy days.

I was still at Ust Vaga when a barishna wearing a short coat, babushka and felt boots arrived with a rig to convey me to Osinova. The weather was bright and pleasant, not quite so cold, and the trip was interesting, especially that I could ride and not plod afoot, as was the case in most of my previous peregrinations all winter.

We were installed in a typical log dwelling which had been im-

Safe from Bolshevik forces and close to supplies from Archangel, members of the 337th Field Hospital Unit gathered for a photograph in front of their Osinova hospital building. Godfrey Anderson is in the front row, second from left. (Ethol Fred Noordman Photo Collection, Polar Bear Expedition Digital Collection, Bentley Historical Library)

provised into a barracks, located just north of the small stream mentioned above. Across the street in a similar building the sergeants were quartered. Just beyond the sergeants' quarters was a block house and a trench. This was manned by a company of Royal Scots, who were quartered farther down the street near the cathedral. There was a daily ritual of changing guards, accompanied by bagpipe music. The Scots wore their blue bonnets and, as the weather moderated, they resumed wearing their tartan kilts and sashes.

Our mess hall was located in a building some 200 yards up the street. All the buildings along the street were huge two-story log structures with a barn attached at the rear and most of them had a runway of poles extending up to the second floor of the barn where hay and flax were stored.

During our sojourn at Osinova there was little practical activity. The action was stalemated and the few casualties were transported to the hospital manned by Section A across the river. We had a sort of

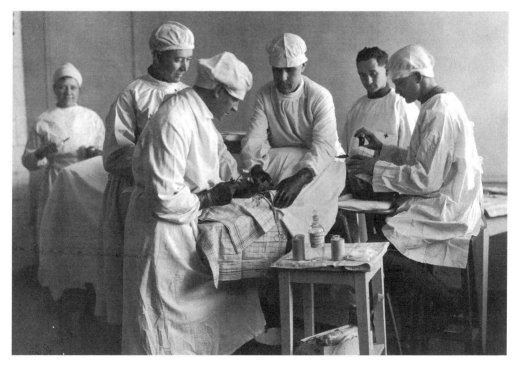

A fully equipped operating room enabled American surgeons in Archangel to care for severely wounded soldiers. (NARS, U.S. Army Signal Corps Photograph, no. SC 161716)

The officers' recovery ward was a well-lit, comfortably equipped space. (NARS, U.S. Army Signal Corps Photograph, no. SC 161722)

first-aid center where our officers were quartered, and there were a couple of good-looking Russian nurses in attendance. The Russian family who had occupied the place we had taken over had moved to a couple of rooms somewhere in the rear. They had a daughter, homely as the proverbial mud fence and without any sex appeal whatsoever, and who was appraised by some of our experts on female pulchritude as "busted a — hole."

We now resumed the setting up exercises and took occasional hikes down the road and across the Dvina to Beresnik and back. Now and then the Scots marched some Bolo prisoners off somewhere through town. Some of our men built a small ski slide down our back yard. Our assistant cook, one Sheiter, claimed that during an altercation, top sergeant Mattson had struck him; so one day the officers and parties concerned drove off somewhere and were gone all day attending a hearing, but nothing came of it. One day Corporal Harter, who

In and around Archangel there was time for outdoor winter recreation activities. American Engineers built a toboggan slide and skating rink. (NARS, Still Picture Collection, no. 161080)

had been up to the Scots' quarters, came back all excited, having picked up the rudiments of chess, and proceeded to teach us. There were some ancient copies of the *London Times* lying around and these carried a chess column, including annotations of games played. I managed to re-play these (on the cardboard outfits and punched out chessman from the Red Cross) but was stumped when I came to the notation "Castles," which Harter hadn't learned and no one knew. There was the usual poker and crap shooting. We had also built a crude four-seat roofed outside latrine. We were issued pack upon pack of cigarettes and chewing gum. The Russian youngsters had got hold of samples of [the latter], and were simply crazy about it, and came around clamoring insistently for "gum-gum-gum."

I remember at Easter time a young British chaplain was sent over and preached a rather perfunctory and lackadaisical sermon. He was apparently just performing an unwelcome assignment. The only thing I remember was that he dwelt upon the word "strength," which he pronounced "strenth," not pronouncing the "g." It was apparent he had no interest in us, talking in an attitude of superiority as to an assembly of uncouth ignoramuses. It must be admitted that his opinion was not altogether unjustified, for one of our crew let a fart in the middle of his dry discourse, which evoked a bit of tittering in the audience.

Spring came on slowly; the weather became milder; the sun rose higher in the heavens; the snow began to thaw and there was much mud and casual water and flooding. The creek crossing the road below our barracks became a good-sized freshet.

One lovely spring day, practically the whole population, accompanied by a couple of priests arrayed in their robes, appeared outside our barracks. And with brooms dipped in water began spraying the building amid various incantations and chants. The purpose of this we could only conjecture, probably to exorcise the devils and evils that had polluted the building during our tenure there. Later the whole assembly went down to the creek and performed some mysterious rituals and ablutions all beyond our comprehension.

A few soldiers found love in Archangel. Private Joseph Chinzi of the 339th Supply Company poses here with his new Russian bride and her family.
(NARS, U.S. Army Signal Corps Photograph, no. SC 159458)

About this time one of our company, a certain Red Oster, came down with the measles and was quarantined in a solitary building down the line. I was chosen as a sort of orderly or companion to tend to the fire and get the chow. It was a soft job with plenty of leisure, and most of the time was spent reading. I still remember one book, Mary Robert Rinehart's "Tish."[5] As the patient improved, we went out for walks. One day, strolling about half a mile south of town we ran into a sort of bayou where a rowboat was tied up and we spent the afternoon exploring, rowing down to the Dvina and back.

Later, when the measles episode was over, Corp. Harter and I went off one day to a wooded glade out of town to do some rifle practice. We had a beltful of clips, each clip holding five shells. We did quite a bit of shooting, after which we continued on to a village some distance beyond. A lot of roofs had weathercocks — the rooster on one end and the arrow pointing on the other. This was too good a target to resist, so we strolled through the town bombarding the weather vanes along the way. Nobody appeared in the street to protest. On our way back we were intercepted by a British squad of four, with rifles slung, and a corporal in charge, ordered out to see what all the firing was about. We were marched back to town, and Harter went on to headquarters to report, but was not long detained and soon returned. When I got back to the barracks I found a number of the boys drunk and boisterous. One of them had shot a hole in my tobacco can standing on a shelf — a foolish thing to do as the Russian family who lived in the rear was more or less in the line of fire.

On the 21st of May the ice broke in the river and for several days the river was full of ice jams piled some twenty feet or more high. In a few days the river was open and the British monitors came up the river to the front and back. The opening of the river and the mud and thawing out of the swamps ended the enemy offensive and events became relatively quiet on all fronts.

Spring now came on with a rush. In no time at all the birches had

---

5. Mystery writer Mary Roberts Rinehart (1876-1958) was sometimes called the American Agatha Christie. She helped her sons Stanley and Frederick, along with John Farrar, found the publishing house Farrar and Rinehart by moving her best-selling mysteries from Doubleday, Doran to their new imprint.

sprouted new leaves and the swamps were arrayed in a delicate green. The days had lengthened and the nights were short. The weather was bland and fair and the sun was out continuously day after day. The people of the village were out in a festive mood, parading up and down the street with their accordions and everyone singing. The youngsters were active on their jump boards and here and there the farmers were scratching the soft earth with their primitive wooden ploughs. The British and Scotch soldiers were playing soccer continuously in a field at the other end of town and sent us a challenge for a game, which we declined, knowing nothing at all about soccer. We had got some baseball equipment, however, and did a little practicing in the evenings. A game was arranged with the engineers across the river at Beresnik and we crossed over to where they had set up a diamond and played the game, but came out somewhat the worse for our efforts. Nothing could be more lovely, I believe, than those halcyon spring days in North Russia, the atmosphere so crystal clear and the air so exhilaratingly fresh and invigorating.

Prior to leaving Archangel, Godfrey Anderson and other baseball-minded soldiers played several games, celebrating their affection for the game and demonstrating it to Russian observers, who were entirely unfamiliar with its rules.   (NARS, U.S. Army Signal Corps Photograph, no. SC 89974)

CHAPTER SEVEN

Archangel to Grand Rapids

Knowledge that they were going home made spring especially beautiful to the American troops in northern Russia. They had been encamped in and around Archangel since February, and as the sunlight, warmth, and budding plants emerged in spring, their mood and health improved. A new American leader, Brigadier General Wilds P. Richardson, arrived on April 17 to prepare them for evacuation. His first step was to designate Economy Point, the location where they had first set foot in Archangel, as the Americans' embarkation station. There, from late May until the end of June, they received medical examinations, packed their luggage, turned in their weapons, and boarded vessels for the trip home. Godfrey Anderson's ship, the *Menominee,* paused briefly at Murmansk and then made its way to Camp Pontanezan near Brest, in northwestern France. There they endured additional bureaucratic procedures, drew their last pay, and had unit photographs taken before boarding a ship to the United States.

The *Great Northern* crossed the Atlantic in less than a week, depositing its passengers in New York just days after President Wilson had returned with the Treaty of Versailles in hand, officially ending World War I and laying the groundwork for a League of Nations, which he promised would avoid future wars. The return of those who were increasingly being referred to as the "Polar Bears" came well over six months after the armistice ending World War I had been signed. Anderson and the other members of that expedition retraced their steps from New York to Detroit, where they received a welcoming parade and celebration. Then it was on to Camp Custer for most of them, the place where they had begun and were now ending their military service. Following their discharge, the soldiers, who had lived and fought together for over a year, made their way home individually or in small groups.

Few people said so at the time, but the Americans' withdrawal from northern Russia in 1919 was an implicit acknowledgment that Woodrow Wilson's intervention policy had been a failure. No such stigma attached to the soldiers. Although their expedition lacked a succinctly stated mission, and they were undermanned and poorly led, the American troops in Russia performed well. When the Great War ended and America's leaders heeded calls to bring all the soldiers home, they returned with their heads held high.

For most Americans, the soldiers' return marked the end of active interest in the war. For Polar Bear veterans, their time in Russia was over — but not ended. They had shared an uncommon experience and had left many of their buddies behind. Authorities had exhumed bodies that were actually buried in the military cemetery in Archangel and returned them with the soldiers. However, many others — missing in action or buried in areas retaken by the Bolsheviks — remained behind. But the returning veterans did not forget. John Cudahy, Joel R. Moore, and Harry H. Mead joined others in founding the Polar Bear Expedition Association in 1922, and served as early presidents. The association's biennial meetings brought veterans together for many years, and even after those veterans had died, second- and third-generation family members and friends continue to hold Memorial Day services at White Chapel Park Cemetery in Troy, Michigan, where a designated area with a white stone sculpture of a polar bear honors the expedition members.[1]

For ten years after they returned, veterans pressured U.S. officials to find a way to bring the bodies of their buddies home. In 1929, Senator Arthur H. Vandenberg of Michigan successfully sponsored legislation allocating $200,000 for the recovery of bodies in northern Russia. Only one problem remained: the United States did not recognize the Soviet Union, so any contact had to be informal. Using private Veterans of Foreign Wars contacts, a small contingent made their way to Archangel and, outfitted

---

1. The Polar Bear Association Web site can be found at http://pbma.grobbel.org/.

as Russian peasants to avoid unwanted publicity, began recovery operations. After two months, eighty-six remains were ready for shipment home. Attended by an honor guard, three sets of remains went to Arlington National Cemetery, and the others went to Detroit for a public ceremony, followed by interment at White Chapel Memorial Park Cemetery. A second expedition recovered nineteen additional bodies in 1934.

Soon after they returned, in 1920, former officers Moore and Mead, assisted by Lewis Mead, another ex-officer, published a history of the expedition: it is entitled *The American Expedition Fighting the Bolsheviki.* Since then, numerous other publications have retold the Polar Bear story. A well-crafted Web site produced by the University of Michigan's Bentley Library staff offers a digital collection of documents and photographs. In 2009, ninety years after they returned, producer/director Pamela Peak produced a documentary video about the expedition entitled "Voices of a Never Ending Dawn."[2] Others produced different forms of unpublished recollections, from brief accounts to photo albums to full-blown memoirs like Godfrey Anderson's. Some of these

A large polar bear sculpture by Leon Hermant stands guard over the graves of Polar Bear Expedition members who are buried at White Chapel Cemetery in Troy, Michigan. (Einar Einarsson Kvaran photo)

personal stories remain in family hands, but many have made their way to archival collections or have been made the core of Web sites. There is a bibliography of books, articles, archival collections, and Web sites at the end of this book. Thanks to this written, visual, and commemorative output, it is unlikely that Americans will soon forget the Polar Bears' exploits. It remains to be seen what lessons they will draw about sending troops to foreign soil.

2. See: http://www.polarbeardocumentary.com/index.html.

"On the way home . . ."

It was somewhere around the first of June that Section B packed their equipment on horse-drawn carts and quit Osinova forever. We crossed the river and set out for the hospital operated by Section A, a mile north of Beresnik. This was our first move on the way home. There were not many patients here now; most had been diverted down the river, transportation being well established now. The hospital consisted of two extensive one-story buildings with several outhouses, including a laundry. There was plenty of room to accommodate Section B, and not much for them to do, so there was plenty of leisure in which to amuse ourselves. There were plenty of books on hand — I remember reading Jack London's "Before Adam" — and there were movies in the British recreation hall in upper Beresnik.[3] I remember an excellent silent movie, "King Lear." The music was furnished by a good trio, violin, cello, and piano. I remember they played, among others, Walter Rolf's "Kiss of Spring."[4] There were baseball games in the flat adjoining lower Beresnik by the river, mostly played in the evening. In fact, where daylight had existed only a few short hours just five months before, now darkness had disappeared and there was continuous daylight. The mosquitoes were legion, large and aggressive. Some of our company would appear in the morning with eyes swollen shut as if they had been stung by bees. For my part I wondered: there being so much syphilis among the Russians, could not a mosquito, after sucking the blood of these syphilitics, transmit the disease by puncturing the blood vessels of anyone attacked by them? For my part, there being several empty rooms in the building at that time, I ap-

3. *Before Adam* thrust evolution into the public spotlight in the early twentieth century and has become a milestone of speculative fiction. In the novel a young man in modern America has visions of an earlier, primitive life. Across the thousands of centuries, his consciousness becomes entwined with that of Big-Tooth, a Pleistocene African ancestor living in a time of perpetual conflict between early humans and protohumans.

4. A 1916 silent version of Shakespeare's famous play, the film starred Frederick Warde, who had played the leading role onstage many times. Unfortunately, Anderson does not comment on his reaction to seeing the play on film without benefit of its dialogue.

Shortly before boarding their ship for the trip home, these soldiers cheered their departure while posing in front of the American flag.   (NARS, Still Picture Collection, no. HD-SN-99-02025)

propriated one of these rooms, cleared it of the pests and slept undisturbed. It was indeed a delightful time, nothing to do, no drills, grand weather, sunny most of the time, and discipline relaxed. There was little activity at the front, and we were all awaiting orders to move.

Finally came the day when a few of us were sent down to lower Beresnik to board a small steamer headed for Archangel. The weather was superb, the air so crystal clear that one could see for miles beyond the river to the infinite distance. On our way we stopped for a moment at a wooded enclosure where the graves of those who had died in the hospital were located. There was the grave of Doughnuts, who had died on the road between Ust Vaga and Beresnik five months before. (Some thirty years later I was to see his grave in the White Chapel cemetery at Bloomfield Hills, near Detroit.)

We boarded the little steamer about mid-morning and in due time we took off and headed downstream. We remained on deck the whole journey and so had a good opportunity to view the impressive scenery

While waiting to depart, soldiers bargained for souvenirs such as samovars, handmade boots, coats, mittens, and hats. (NARS, U.S. Army Signal Corps Photograph, no. SC 161696)

along the way. In the evening — there was no nightfall — we bedded down on the deck and fell at once into deep slumber, undisturbed until we awoke the next morning in the brilliant sunshine. We arrived at Archangel around noon and put up at quarters near the riverfront. Archangel was greatly transformed from what it had been when we left it the year before. The main streets were swarming with a great variety of civilians and soldiers in different styles of uniforms. The streetcars were running, operated by women; no fares were collected from the military, as far as I could see. Our entire company was soon fully assembled, and were busy getting their equipment together, and the officers were painting directions on their luggage.

It was on the evening of the second day when we finally assembled and lined up in the street below, and began our march down toward the waterfront. There were many people in the streets and from the upper windows along the way the whores of Archangel gave the Yanks a fond and noisy farewell.

The transport was moored alongside the dock; it was the *Menominee,* which had bucked through the broken ice floe, with two other ships following in its wake. We climbed the gangplank, then went below, each to appropriate a hammock and deposit his luggage underneath. Then we returned to the deck to take a last look at the memorable and never-to-be-forgotten prospect spread out before us. On the near side lay Archangel, no longer the dead town we had visited the year before, its ornate public buildings and splendid cathedrals stretching away in both directions; the wide expanse of the river; and far across the bay, historic Bakaritza sprawled along the horizon.

Finally, everyone aboard and everything made ready, the *Menominee* was eased out of its moorings and out into midstream, and headed for the main channel through the delta. We passed Economy Point and in due time were threading our way through that interminable maze of morass and swamp grass that extended in every direction as far as the eye could reach.

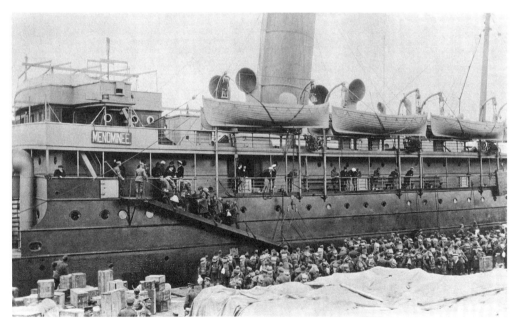

In early summer, 1919, Godfrey Anderson and his fellow American soldiers boarded the USS *Menominee* for the trip back to the United States. (NARS, U.S. Army Signal Corps Photograph, no. SC 89989)

As night descended, if you could call it night, we went below and hit the hammocks, as it were, happy to abandon the view of dreary desolation. We woke betimes in the morning and went up out of that foul-smelling hold to get a breath of fresh air. We were out of sight of all land. The weather was dark and gloomy and there was a brisk, chilling wind that gave one the shivers.

After a couple of days the weather brightened; about this time we were entering the passage that led to Kola Bay at the end of which sprawled Murmansk, where we drew up alongside a long wharf.

Murmansk, from what we could see of it, seemed to be less of the usual inhabited town than a sort of supply depot with an extensive dock area, littered with quonsets, hoisting derricks, warehouses and other buildings, several side tracks, a couple of rows of box cars, and odds and ends of what looked like junk strewn about.[5] The weather here was mild, and though it was late in the evening the sun shone brilliantly. The company disembarked and went for a long hike around the area. The next day there was a little trouble with the Limeys. It so happened that our ship was moored at one corner of a square dock. Around the corner at right angles, a British transport full of Limeys was moored. Both sides began catcalling and exchanging insults, and presently they began throwing various missiles at each other — whatever was at hand. Some Yanks even unscrewed nuts from the hoisting and other machinery. One fellow had an orange, which he did not hesitate to heave. Before it was over the Limeys were forced to retreat out of range. At another time the boys engaged in a furious pillow fight, as it were, using instead of pillows, those soft life preservers. After a day or so at Murmansk we resumed our journey and moved out into the Arctic Ocean again. It seemed strange to travel all night as if in daylight. I got up one night at 2 a.m. to go to the latrine. The sun was swinging along the horizon, due north. The midnight sun, they called it.

A couple of our crew were taken into custody, having been caught

---

5. The buildings Anderson saw were semicircular corrugated steel-surfaced Nissen Huts developed by the British major Peter Norman Nissen in 1916. The 100,000 produced for the British army in World War I became the prototype for Quonset Huts, which were produced for the U.S. Army in World War II. Frederick W. J. McCosh, *Nissen of the Huts: A Biography of Lt. Col. Peter Nissen, DSO* (Bourne End, UK: B. D. Publishing, 1997), pp. 82-108.

smoking cigarettes in a haymow in the ship. (It had been transporting mules.)

Those were relaxing, restful days as we traversed along the Norway coast well within the sight of land, all serrated and indented with craggy fiords. The weather remained delightful all the way.

After several days the ship swerved to the southwest and passed between the Orkneys and Scotland, and a bit later we entered the Irish Sea and passed along the east coast of Ireland, so close indeed that we were almost within a stone's throw, it seemed, of those ancient round towers that we passed.[6] Toward sunset we passed Lands End and later there was a bit of singing. "Just a Baby's Prayer at Twilight" was one, as the moon rose grandly along the eastern horizon, and finally everyone went below to sleep out the last night of the voyage.[7] When we awoke the next morning we were anchored in Brest harbor.

With time on their hands aboard ship, several members of the 337th Field Hospital climbed onto the rigging for a group photo. (Ethol Fred Noordman Photo Collection, Polar Bear Expedition Digital Collection, Bentley Historical Library, University of Michigan)

6. The "round towers" Anderson refers to are early medieval stone towers, ranging in height from 50 to more than 100 feet high, found mainly in Ireland. They may have been bell towers or places to retreat for refuge, or a combination of both.

7. "Just a Baby's Prayer at Twilight (For Her Daddy Over There)," words by Sam Lewis and Joe Young, music by M. K. Jerome, was published by the Waterson, Berlin & Snyder Co. in the closing year of the war, 1918. Its opening lyrics are:

> I've heard the prayers of mothers
> Some of them old and gray
> I've heard the prayers of others
> For those who went away.
>
> Oft times a prayer will teach one
> The meaning of good bye
> I felt the pain of each one,
> But this one made me cry
> Just a baby's prayer at twilight . . .

The ocean-going ships cannot dock at Brest but must stop out in the harbor and the passengers must transfer to a ferry boat to reach shore.

The 337th disembarked at a dock in Brest and passing through a huge warehouse emerged to a street leading through a part of the city to a camp near the outskirts. This camp, Pontanezan, consists of tents laid out in parallel rows, with board walks between (it was muddy when wet).[8] The camp was quite extensive. There were trucks to pick up the garbage cans, which were handled by German prisoners. There were camp followers — prostitutes — dressed in their best finery, strolling about in pairs. There was a permanent bleacher or scaffolding where the various outgoing companies were arranged to be photographed. I suppose that every company at Pontanezan before heading for home had their picture taken here.

We were in Camp Pontanezan at the time when President Wilson was in Paris during the peace talks, and it so happened that he arrived in Brest and embarked for home a day or so before we were scheduled to leave.[9] When that day finally came we retraced our steps and marched back down to the docks. In passing down a busy street we were intrigued by the public latrines along the way. Beside a stone wall the citizen could relieve himself behind a panel along the sidewalk that concealed only that part of him between the shoulders and knees.

It was a bit later in the afternoon when we got aboard the large ferry boat that conveys passengers out to the transports anchored in the harbor. We pulled out into the harbor, but our transport had not yet come in. We waited around until midnight before it [the transport vessel *Great Northern*] came in and dropped anchor and we clambered

8. Camp Pontanezan in Brest was initially the major U.S. replacement depot in France. At the war's conclusion, it became the major debarkation point for U.S. troops on their way home. Benjamin R. Beede, ed., *The War of 1898 and U.S. Interventions, 1898-1934: An Encyclopedia* (New York: Garland Publishing, 1994), pp. 80-81.

9. Wilson was headed home with the Treaty of Versailles officially ending all hostilities between the Allied nations and Germany, assigning blame for the war to Germany and requiring it to pay reparations, and creating the League of Nations, which he believed would prevent another conflict like the war just ended. When he got home, Wilson encountered U.S. Senate opposition to his country's participation in the League. Despite Wilson's strenuous promotion of its merits, the Senate ultimately failed to ratify the treaty.

aboard. As soon as we were assigned our hammocks, I, for one, was soon asleep.

When I awoke in the morning we were far out at sea, which was quite agitated and choppy. There were other units aboard and a few of these had married French girls. Some of these girls were miserably seasick, and their husbands were constantly escorting them to the latrine assigned to them. After a day or so the seas calmed down. One day there was a great hullabaloo as a great iceberg was seen floating in the near distance. Some of the ship's crew took pictures of it, which they developed and made a brisk sale of the prints. On the fourth of July we got reports of the Dempsey-Willard prizefight.[10] All during those mild days the decks were literally crowded with soldiers sprawled about so thickly that one could scarcely make his way through the congestion. In one corner a group of colored boys kept up a continuous crap game.

The *Great Northern* was a fast ship. It took just five and a half days to reach New York. When we passed the *Ambrose Light* ship in the late afternoon everyone was standing crowded (some had climbed into the rigging), all looking in one direction for a first glimpse of the good old U.S.A.

Before long we entered the Lower Bay, then past the Statue of Liberty and the Battery Park, and finally docked somewhere at Hoboken. Then we entrained for a place farther up the river called Camp Merritt, with the usual wooden barracks. After a day we slung our packs aboard a train and headed north to Albany, then across the state to Buffalo, across Canada and arrived at Detroit after dark. Here we stopped for a short time, where we got an enthusiastic reception. Some of the Detroit boys were met by wives, sweethearts and parents, and there were some tearful reunions. After a while we reboarded the train and proceeded on through the night to Camp Custer, where we were quartered in a barracks. The next day or so we went through a medical check up, turned in our government equipment and posed for another picture and got our discharges. Then it was all over. I boarded the Kalamazoo

10. Jack Dempsey became heavyweight boxing champion in Toledo, Ohio, on July 4, 1919, when then titleholder Jess Willard failed to answer the bell for the fourth round.

When they returned to Detroit, a downtown parade and a Belle Isle picnic welcomed the men of the 339th Infantry and 337th Field Hospital Unit. (Wayne State University, Reuther Archives, *Detroit News* Photograph Collection 77762_3JP2-wi-he-re1-xo-yo-sw-sh-r0-final.jpg)

interurban and hit Grand Rapids at dusk and transferred to the Muskegon interurban and got off at the county line where my parents were waiting to greet me.[11] It was about ten o'clock, and it was good to be home again, with gratitude to God for bringing us back safely.

It was a couple of days later that we read in the paper that President Wilson, aboard the *George Washington*, had arrived in the States.

11. Although the city of Grand Rapids offered no homecoming celebration for the soldiers who had served in Russia, Grand Rapids newspapers did provide front-page coverage of their return and lists of returning soldiers. In all of the coverage, reference is to the 339th Infantry Regiment; none of the articles mentions the 337th Hospital Unit, continuing right to the end of the expedition the confusion that got the 337th assigned to Russia in the first place.

Godfrey Anderson's Legacy

THE COUNTRY TO WHICH the "Polar Bears" returned had undergone significant changes in their absence. A more realistic appreciation of the horrors and consequences of war had supplanted the confident patriotism that had sent them on their mission a year earlier. Citizens, as they dealt with messages from their family members at the front, as well as with wartime shortages and rationing, questioned the merit of intervening in European disputes. By the time the soldiers of the North Russia Expedition finally returned, the mood had shifted in Grand Rapids and around the nation: postwar readjustment had replaced war fever, and most of the Polar Bears' fellow draftees had readjusted to civilian life. Anxious about a furniture workers' strike and charges of corruption in local government before the war, voters had adopted a new city charter and elected a new mayor in 1916. Though the city's furniture industry was still struggling to recover from a downturn caused by the strike and exacerbated by the war years, Grand Rapids faced the 1920s with optimism.

Like much of the rest of the nation, local residents wanted to put the war in the rearview mirrors of the cars they were now buying in increasing numbers. When President Woodrow Wilson brought home a peace treaty ending the war and creating the League of Nations to adjudicate future international disagreements, Grand Rapidians, like many of their countrymen, viewed the proposal with skepticism. They wanted peace but not involvement, hoping that the broad Atlantic would isolate them from future European conflagrations. Although they welcomed Godfrey Anderson and his compatriots when they came home, few wanted to see any continuation of the kind of foreign involvement that had taken American soldiers to northern Russia. Beyond their fellow veterans and members of their families, the returning soldiers found little interest in the Polar Bears' remarkable adventure — and even less enthusiasm for any future entanglements.

When Godfrey Anderson returned home, he wasted little time picking up the life he had left a year earlier. Ruth Anderson (her last name before their marriage was also Anderson) had accepted his marriage proposal before he left, and after he returned they planned to marry as soon as he had a good job. His first job was with the well-known Berkey and Gay Furniture Company, where he spent a year gluing dresser drawers before he learned of a better-paying position ($.35 per hour, 50 hours per week) doing more demanding drawer-fitting work for the highly regarded Johnson-Handley-Johnson Furniture Company. Godfrey and Ruth Anderson married soon after he began this new job, and they settled into a home on Grand Rapids' West Side. Anderson stayed with the Johnson company until his retirement forty-five years later. The couple's only child, Robert, was born in 1925. When time permitted, Godfrey continued his interest in history, slowly building a personal Abraham Lincoln and Civil War library, as well as studying the history of Swedish immigrants in West Michigan.

Throughout their lives, Godfrey and Ruth Anderson were active members of the First Evangelical Covenant Church of Grand Rapids, a predominantly Swedish congregation. True to his interest in history, Anderson was a member of the church's archives committee, and he organized its written and photographic records. He also prepared a history of the church's founding, entitled "Early Days in the Swedish Mission Movement in Grand Rapids."

Later in life, Anderson became increasingly interested in local history, and he began building a large photograph collection. One of his largest undertakings was the documentation of the Grand River, Michigan's longest, from its source near Jackson to its outlet in Lake Michigan at Grand Haven. Over the course of several years he traveled the course of the river, photographing its every crossing from all direc-

tions and carefully describing the location. He slept in his car on overnight trips. Ultimately, the project filled eighteen three-ring binders.
Similarly, he created a collection of more than 400 black-and-white
photographs of Grand Rapids in the 1950s and 1960s, including many
documenting the downtown area affected by urban renewal.

Anderson also created a ten-notebook collection of other Grand
Rapids photographs and documents. He copied historical photographs
and then carefully researched the details in each. A similar collection
of photographs from the Sparta area grew to more than 750 images.
Complementing the photographic material were several research and
writing efforts, including two on Swedish Christmas customs in West
Michigan: "Christmas as the Old-Time Swedes Observed It" (1965)
and "Christmas in the Country and the Yulefest at Axel Carlson's"
(1966). At the time of his death, he had completed the first drafts of a
broader history of the area's Swedish community, as well as a history of
Sparta.

Anderson's best work, however, was his memoir of his service with
the Allied North Russia Expeditionary Force. As with all his other
work, he wrote clearly and accurately of the experience, especially the
difficult retreat from Shenkursk through the frozen Russian night.
Previous to the publication of this book, portions of his memoir were
published in 1982 in Dennis Gordon's book *Quartered in Hell: The Story
of the American North Russian Expeditionary Force, 1918-1919;* and a
short segment of the memoir appeared as an article, "The Polar Bears:
A Memoir," in the *Grand River Valley Review* (vol. 4, no. 1, Fall/Winter
1982), a journal published by the Grand Rapids Historical Society. Anderson also left a recorded interview in the local history collection at
the Grand Rapids Public Library.

Anderson's recollections of the soldiers' departure from England
and their arrival in Archangel, when the entire vessel was plagued by
Spanish flu and, because of either negligence or a shipping mix-up, had
virtually no medicines, give very personal testimony to that devastating
viral pandemic. Similarly, his descriptions of setting up hospitals in
Archangel and further up the Dvina and Vaga rivers, including events
such as the Christmas party the soldiers sponsored for the residents of
Shenkursk, provide a view in microcosm of the hospital unit's work
and its social activities.

These descriptions make Godfrey Anderson's memoir a useful contribution to the literature of the North Russia Expedition, even without his harrowing account of the Bolsheviks' winter offensive and of the U.S. Army's nightmarish retreat along a frozen back trail from Shenkursk to the village of Beresnik and eventually to Osinova, near Archangel. That narrative raises his account to a higher level as a war memoir. Encroaching Bolshevik fighters nearly cut off the Allied soldiers, who were transporting the wounded from the Shenkursk hospital, and only the help of their supporters in the village and the discovery of a seldom-used, unguarded trail enabled them to avoid being surrounded and cut off — as some of their comrades had been in more remote encampments. Anderson provides a memorable description of the loading of wounded onto small sleighs pulled by tiny Russian ponies and stealthily slipping into the surrounding forest as enemy artillery opened up on the town. From there the fleeing caravan made its torturous way through deep snow to the Dvina River, and then north to the relative safety provided by the garrisons closer to Archangel.

Godfrey Anderson wrote his memoir so that future generations would remember the men he served with and cared for. Although he was well versed in American history and wrote his memoir in the aftermath of the Vietnam War, Anderson chose not to compare his time in Russia to other U.S. interventions of the twentieth century. In more ways than one, Anderson exemplified his country's ideal of a citizen soldier. He began his military service as a draftee who did his duty and accepted the orders he received. When superiors selected him and several others to serve in a hospital unit, he accepted the work without complaint, caring for his comrades to the best of his ability. When orders came down to prepare for transport to Russia, he did not question the order. At each step, he accepted the decisions of his officers and did his duty. Even when his memoir deals with the decision to leave Russia, he plays the role of historical reporter presenting the facts without judgment. Perhaps most importantly, he told his story — and the story of his comrades-in-arms — in the hope that it would evoke the recognition that it richly deserved. And in telling that story Anderson provided an invaluable resource for those seeking to understand a soldier's life in the North Russia Expedition.

AT THE TIME of his death, April 23, 1981, Godfrey Anderson had made arrangements to place most of his history materials with libraries in Illinois and Michigan. His library of Lincoln and Civil War books went to North Park College (now University) in Chicago, a Christian liberal arts school founded in 1891 by the Evangelical Covenant Church. Manuscript copies of his memoir are located in the Bentley Historical Library at the University of Michigan and the Grand Rapids Public Library's local history collection. The remainder of his historical photographic albums and manuscripts went to the Grand Rapids Public Library as well.

Anderson clearly understood that he had participated in an important historical event when his government sent him to Russia. He also understood that if such events were the warp of historical fabric, then its weft was the everyday life of his fellow citizens, their ceremonies and customs, their businesses, schools and places of worship, and the structures where they live and work. He would take great pleasure in knowing that his dedication to preserving the history he knew and experienced earned the appreciation and respect of area researchers who regularly consult the materials he produced.

Liverpool to Brookwood Station

Godfrey Anderson wrote a brief travel narrative of the English countryside through which the troop train passed. He did not know the historical details at the time he and his fellow soldiers traveled through England, but he studied the route after his war experience had ended. Much of his information about the English countryside came from his visits to the Grand Rapids Public Library, where he researched subjects of general history, as well as local history, throughout his adult life. The descriptions in Appendices A and B are an indication of Anderson's interest in history and his desire to fully understand and describe his brief stay in England as part of his larger military experience. His travel narrative begins as the troop train pulls out of Liverpool.

WHAT LITTLE WE SAW of Liverpool in passing were mostly clusters of ancient looking red brick buildings. Most of us fell into a fitful doze, despite the unearthly scream of the locomotive's whistle at frequent intervals. The Midland Railroad coincides with the Manchester, Liverpool and Northwestern R.R. and heads straight east toward Manchester [for twenty miles]. At the town of Glazehook, twenty-five miles to the east, the Midland R.R. diverges to the south. At about thirteen miles farther south there is a railroad intersection at Stockport. At Marple, forty-three miles farther, we entered Derbyshire where the hills of the Peak District are visible to the left. We passed Chinley and then just beyond Chapel-on-the-Firth (fifty-two miles) the train enters the Doveholes Tunnel, one and a half miles long. All this area is rocky hill country. At sixty miles we entered the romantic Valley of the Wye, the view here the most attractive on the line. Here the train passes through two tunnels. Farther on beyond the Longstons Tunnel, at sixty-six miles, we reached Bake-well, a delightfully situated village of fewer than 3,000 inhabitants. Be-yond is another tunnel. A little past the village of Rousley, at seventy miles, the Wye flows into the Derwent River whose broad valley we now followed. Just beyond Matlock, at some seventy-five miles, the train passes through the High Tor Tunnel. Just beyond this the train threads through another long tunnel beyond which is Cromfort, at seventy-six miles, Ambergalt, eighty-one miles, and Belper, eighty-four miles.

Here we quit the hilly district and entered the wide plain of central England. At ninety-one miles from Liverpool the train crossed the Derwent River and came to a temporary stop at the station at Derby. It must have been around midnight when we came to Derby. Here we were served refreshments — just what, I can't remember. We could not see much of this town — its population very well over 100,000 — but we recalled some of its past history. Wm. the Conqueror presented the town to his natural son "Peveril of the Peak" (Scott wrote a novel by this name) but the relics of his castle are long gone. Also Derby was the most southerly point reached by the Pretender Chas. Stuart and his Highlanders on their attempted march to London in 1745. Samuel Richardson, author of the first novel, "Clarrissa Harlow," and Herbert Spenser the philosopher were born here. The first silk mill in England was erected at Derby in 1718 on an island in the Derwent.

Two principal lines of the Midland R.R. diverge at Derby, one to the SW via Birmingham and the other to the SE by way of Leicester to London. Indeed the whole of Britain is crisscrossed by a vast and com-plicated network of railroad[s] proceeding in all directions. From Derby we traversed the second line mentioned. After following the Derwent valley some ten miles beyond Derby to Trent Junction the R.R. crosses the Trent River, and then follows the Soar Valley to

Loughborough (close to 25,000 population) which contains a large bell foundry where the bell in St. Paul's Cathedral was cast in 1882. Still following the Soar Valley past the village of Syston it reaches the ancient town of Leicester, some one hundred twenty miles from Liverpool, a place of some 225,000 inhabitants. Its history goes back a long way. It was a site of Roman activities and a Roman wall still exists, besides many relics, and pavement bricks have been unearthed. Tradition ascribed the original foundation of Leicester to King Lear.[1] Cardinal [Thomas] Wolsey died in Leicester Abbey in 1530. The Lady Jane Grey was born near here.

Four miles beyond Leicester at Wigston three branch lines diverge to Nuneaton, to Birmingham and to Rugby. Twelve miles further on is a small town, a great hunting center, called Market Harborough, probably of Roman origin, with traces of a Roman camp in the vicinity. Charles I had his headquarters here before the Battle of Naseby, 1645. (Naseby lies seven miles to the southwest.) Eleven miles beyond is the town of Kettering, of nearly 30,000 inhabitants. The train follows the Ise [River] some seven miles to Wellingborough and three miles to Ecton, the birthplace of Benj. Franklin's father (the house was visited by Benj. Franklin in 1758). From here the train enters the valley of the winding Ouse, which we crossed six times before reaching Bedford, a town with a population approaching 40,000, and one hundred seventy miles from Liverpool. The town was apparently occupied before the Roman period. Of special interest in Bedford are the mementos of John Bunyan, author of "Pilgrims Progress." He was born in Elston, one mile to the south. He was confined for twelve years in the Bedford gaol and during a subsequent incarceration of six months some three years later he wrote "Pilgrims Progress." In a public square stands a bronze statue of Bunyan. Bedford is quite a R.R. center; lines extend thru Cambridge, Northampton, Oxford and one to London. The Midland R.R. on which we traveled bypassed London on the west.

A few miles S. of Bedford the train crosses the Ouse and traverses a flat and fertile district, then passed through another tunnel before

---

1. Legend has it that Leir, the mythical king of the Britons, founded the city of Kaerleir ("Leir's chester," i.e., fortified town). Shakespeare's *King Lear* is loosely based on the king's story.

reaching the small town of Ampthill, near which is the site of an old castle where Catherine of Aragon resided during her trial.

Thirteen miles further on the train passes thru Luton, a town of more than 50,000 inhabitants famous for its manufacture of straw hats. Ten miles further on we reached St. Albans, a town of over 20,000. This town was named after St. Alban, a Roman soldier, a Christian martyr executed here in AD 304, the first Christian martyr in Britain. A short distance to the west is the site of Verulamium, the most important town in the south of England during the Roman period, where fragments of the walls still remain.[2] St. Albans was the scene of two of the battles fought during the Wars of the Roses: the first in 1455 and the second was fought in 1461 just north of the town. Some eight miles beyond St. Albans is the town of Edgware. Near here is the village of Whitechurch where Handel was organist and choirmaster in the church from 1718-21. A blacksmith shop in Edgware is said to be the place where Handel conceived the idea of his "Harmonious Blacksmith."

At Edgware a branch of the R.R. diverges to London while the mainline bypasses London to the west. Our route along here was somewhat wooded but far in the distance we could catch glimpses now and then of the great metropolis. At one point about ten miles beyond Edgware we crossed the Thames River, not very wide nor prepossessing at this point. The line we were on terminates some ten miles beyond this point at Croydon. However, at a point some five miles before reaching the termination, we were diverted over on the South Western Railroad and proceeded from this junction some seven miles to the village of Esher, located not far south of the Thames River, celebrated in the verses of Pope and Thomas. In this vicinity once stood the palace of Cardinal Wolsey. Nearby is Claremont, once the property of Lord Clive,[3] inhabited at a later period by the Princess Charlotte (who died here in 1817) and her husband Leopold, King of All Belgians.[4] It was

2. Initially an Iron Age settlement, Verulamium was the third largest city in Roman Britain. A portion of the Roman city, now park and agricultural land, remains unexcavated.

3. Major General Robert Clive, First Baron Clive of Plassey, 1725-1774, also known as Clive of India, is credited with establishing the military and political supremacy of the East India Company in Southern India and Bengal.

4. Princess Charlotte Augusta of Wales (1796-1817) was the only child produced

afterward the residence of Louis Philippe and his wife, both of whom died there.[5] Nearly five miles further southwest is the village of Weybridge. Nearby is St. Georges Hill, which commands a beautiful view which includes the North Windsor Castle and Hampton Court. Nearly six miles beyond [that] the railroad passes Woking. At Woking is a Convict Prison for invalid prisoners and the Necropolis, an immense cemetery two thousand acres in extent to which a special funeral train runs every day from London. Three miles further on is the village of Brookwood Station, a little beyond which a loop line diverges to Aldershot (seven and a half miles) and terminates at Winchester, thirty-five miles distant.

[Brookwood Station, the destination for Anderson's troop train, is about thirty miles southwest of London, with a large Army camp close by. During their brief stay there, he and several of his 337th Hospital Unit mates received brief hospital training at the British military hospital a few miles away in Aldershot.]

---

by the ill-fated marriage of George IV and Caroline of Brunswick. Had she lived, Charlotte would have been queen of the United Kingdom. She married Prince Leopold of Saxe-Coburg-Saalfeld in 1816 at Carlton House; but she died in childbirth in November 1817.

5. Louis Philippe (1773-1850) reigned as the French king from 1830 to 1848. During the February 1848 Revolution, he abdicated the throne and fled with his family to England, where he and his wife, Amelia, lived until their deaths.

Brookwood Station to Newcastle

Anderson's second train ride through England took him from Brookwood Station north to Newcastle. Once again, he used the opportunity to diverge from his memoir and write a description of the countryside through which he passed.

OUR STAY IN ENGLAND had been interesting, the weather delightful, at times a bit hot. I do not remember that it rained once during our stay there. We now retraced the same route we had traversed before until we reached St. Albans, finally connecting up with the Great Northern Railroad somewhere north of that city. About where we recrossed the Thames we got a brief glimpse of London far in the distance to the east. I can still remember seeing the white dome of St. Paul's looming in solitary grandeur atop a far off eminence. All afternoon we passed through central England with its many sites famous in English history. . . .

From St. Albans the branch of the R.R. diverted us to the northeast some three miles to Hatfield, a small market town on the Lea

River, where we joined the Great Northern R.R. In Hatfield are the ruins of a twelfth century royal residence or palace [part of the Royal Manor at Woodstock], where Queen [then Princess] Elizabeth was confined by her half sister Queen Mary and where she received news of her accession to the throne. King Charles I was also imprisoned here for a short time.[1]

Fourteen miles to the north is Hitchin, a small country town where branch lines diverge to Cambridge and Bedford. About thirteen miles beyond at Sandy (the old Roman Salinae) we crossed the London and Northwest line from Oxford to Cambridge. Beyond Sandy the railroad parallels the Ouse River which it crosses, after passing thru the hamlets of Saint Neots and Offord some fifteen miles from where it crosses the river at Huntingdon, a small town of some 4,000 inhabitants. It is noted chiefly as the birthplace of Oliver Cromwell (1599). The poet [William] Cowper [1731-1800] lived here at one time. Some sixteen or seventeen miles beyond we reached Peterborough (pop. 30,000) after traversing the flat district known as the Fens and passing a village called Holme where a branch connects it with Ramsey and St. Ives. Peterborough, situated on the Nene, is an ancient city, noted mostly for its cathedral, 471 feet long, one of the most important Norman churches left in England. The present building is the third church on this site. The first, founded in 656, was destroyed by the Danes in 870. The second was founded in 971 and burned down in 1116, the present building erected in the latter 12th century. Here is buried Queen Catherine of Aragon (d. 1548), and Mary Queen of Scots (beheaded 1587) was buried here (later reburied in Westminster Abbey).

About half way between Peterborough and Essender (12 miles) we crossed the Welland River. At Essender a branch line diverges to

---

1. Woodstock Manor was the site of a royal residence since the twelfth century, where the future Queen Elizabeth I was held for a time. At the beginning of the eighteenth century, Queen Anne gave the manor and estate to John Churchill, first Duke of Marlborough, in gratitude for his victory at Blenheim on the Danube River against the French and Bavarian armies, and she promised to pay for the building of a new house on the site. Finished more than twenty years later, the new Blenheim Palace was the birthplace of future Prime Minister Winston Churchill in November 1874. *A History of the County of Oxford: Wootton Hundred (South) including Woodstock*, vol. 12 (1990), pp. 431-435. URL: http://www.british-history.ac.uk/report.aspx?compid=7523.

Stamford on the left and Lincoln on the right. About five miles to the NE is Bourn where the Saxon Hereward made a desperate stand against William the Conqueror. Seventeen miles farther on is Grantham, an ancient town (pop. about 18,000). Sir Isaac Newton attended grammar school here (there is a statue of him in the square). King John is said to have held a court here in 1213 and it is here that Richard III signed the death warrant of the Duke of Buckingham. Five miles to the north at Burkstone a branch line diverges on the right to Boston and Lincoln. Eleven miles further is Newark-on-Trent, an old town of some 16,000 population. King John died here in 1216. The old castle (12th century) which stood here sustained three sieges during the Civil War and was then dismantled.

We crossed the Trent and at some twelve miles further north we passed Tuxford where the line from Chesterfield to Lincoln crosses the Great Northern Railroad. Some six or seven miles further on we reached the village of Retford, a junction of lines leading to Sheffield, Hull and Lincoln. Eight miles beyond is the village of Scrooby. William Brewster, a ruling elder of the Pilgrim Fathers, was born here. A couple of miles further on we passed Bawtry, the birthplace of William Bradford, the second governor of the Colony of Plymouth in America. Another eight miles brought us to Doncaster (pop. about 46,000). The town appeared begrimed and sooty, and was home to the works of the Great Northern R.R. Lines run from here to Sheffield, Manchester and Liverpool, to Wakefield, Leeds, Pontefract and York, Goole and Hull and Gainsborough and Lincoln. Thirteen miles further north at Snaith the Great Northern and two other lines intersect, one from the west (Wakefield) and one from the SW, both headed for Hull.

Approaching Selby (pop. about 85,000) some six miles farther on we crossed the Ouse River two or three times, the town lying on the river Selby. It is said to be the birthplace of Henry I. Near the station is the Abbey Church, one of the finest monastic churches in England. The Leeds to Hull line runs through Selby and a branch diverts to Market Weighton. Fourteen miles further on we arrive at York, a city of more than 75,000 people, situated on the Ouse River. York is the Eboracum of the Romans, their chief province in Britain, the headquarters of the 6th Legion and the frequent residence of the Emperor. Septimus Severus died and was buried in York in 311 and Constantine the Great was proclaimed emperor here in 306.[2] York was the center from which Christianity spread thru Northern England. It was an important Danish colony during their occupation. Wm. the Conqueror built two castles here and the town is connected with innumerable important events in English history. York Minster is one of the largest and grandest cathedrals in England (525 ft. long, 100 ft. high, 110 ft. wide across the nave, 222 ft. across the transepts). The earliest church on this site was a small wooden one (627), and [was] soon replaced by a stone basilica which burned in the 8th century. A third church was burned down in 1069 by Wm. the Conqueror. A fourth was built on the same site by a Norman bishop and was not completed in its present form until late in the 15th century.

The city is partly surrounded by walls built about the middle of the 14th century, partly on the line of the old Roman walls. There is a so-called Norman mound, the site of Wm. the Conqueror's second castle. Beyond the [Ouse] river is the original castle, now a prison, where the infamous massacre of five hundred Jews took place during the reign of Richard I (1189-99). About six miles to the west is Marston Moor, where Cromwell defeated the Royalists in 1644.

While I was at Stoney Castle Camp I had borrowed a book at the servicemen's library there, namely [Charles] Dickens' "Nicholas Nickleby." This I had been perusing off and on, on that long all day journey toward the north of England. It so happened that I was reading about Schoolmaster Squiers and his infamous Yorkshire Dotheboys school as Dickens described it at the very time we were passing through that same county of Yorkshire.

Just beyond York we crossed the Ouse again and four miles beyond lies Skelton where a line from Harrogate to Market Weighton crosses the Great Northern line. Sixteen miles north of York we passed through Pilmoor village where another line crosses the Great Northern, that from Knaresborough (to the left) and to Malton on the right. Five miles east of Pilmoor is the village of Coxwold where [Laurence] Sterne wrote "Tristram Shandy" and "Sentimental Journey," while some five miles to the west is Aldborough built on the site of the Roman city of *Isurium*.

---

2. York was founded in AD 71, when Rome's Ninth Legion constructed a fort at the site. Roman archaeological remains include remnants of the headquarters building, a bath, temple, bridge, and portions of the city wall.

Some seven miles further on is Thirsk, a small country town of perhaps 5,000 population where a branch line connects with Harrogate and Leeds. Continuing seven miles further we reached Northallerton, a town of some 4,300 inhabitants, located three miles south of the site of the Battle of the Standard (1138), a busy R.R. center. A line crosses here leading to Stockton and Hartlepool to the northeast and to Leyburn and Hawes to the west. Nine miles farther on is the village of Dalton from which a branch line runs to Richmond to the west.

Another six miles brought us to Darlington, a busy town of more than 55,000 inhabitants. The first passenger line in the country, the Stockton and Darlington Railway, was opened here in 1825. The first locomotive used on that line is preserved at the station in a glass house. There is a branch line west to Tebay. Another runs northwest to Bishop Auckland, others to the east to Stockton and Middlesbrough. Another fourteen miles, at Ferryhill Junction, branch lines run to Hartlepool, Bishop Aukland and Coxhoe.

Nine miles further on we arrived at Durham, population about 16,000, an ancient town, the older and most important part of which is situated on an [island] of the Wear River, almost surrounded by a horseshoe loop of the river. Durham at an earlier time suffered severely from the inroads of Scottish borderers. The Durham Cathedral is one of the most important and most grandly situated of English cathedrals — 510 ft. long, 80 ft. wide, 170 ft. across the transepts and 70 ft. [in] height. The central tower is 214 ft. high. [It is] believed to contain the remains of the Venerable Bede (d. 735).[3] The castle at Durham was built by Wm. the Conqueror in 1072, now occupied by Durham University. From Durham a line runs to Sunderland to the NE and another to Bishop Auckland to the SW.

Shortly after leaving Durham (six miles) we reached Chester-le-Street, an ancient town supposed to lie on the site of the Roman *Condercum*.[4] Another five or six miles brought us to Gateshead, a large

3. The Venerable Bede (ca. 672-735) was a Benedictine monk who was well known as an author and scholar. His most famous work, *Historia Ecclesiastica Gentis Anglorum* (*The Ecclesiastical History of the English People*), gained him the title "Father of English History."

4. Condercum was the site of a fort constructed between AD 122 and 124, and was an associated small settlement on Hadrian's Wall (www.roman-britain.org/places/condercum.htm).

and uninteresting manufacturing town (pop. more than 90,000) located on the south bank of the Tyne, practically a suburb of Newcastle.

Newcastle occupies the site of the Roman *Pons Aelius;* in Saxon times it was named Monk Chister.[5] The present name is derived from the castle built in the 11th century by the eldest son of Wm. the Conqueror. On the platform of the Central Station is preserved Stephenson No. 1 engine and a bit beyond is a statue of George Stephenson (d. 1848). George Stephenson built his first locomotive at Killingworth, six miles north of Newcastle.

As the road curves as it approaches the Tyne River we got a magnificent view of the High Level Bridge crossing the river and the station just beyond, and the city of Newcastle (population about 250,000) which lies on the left or north bank of the river. The High Level Bridge is a triumph of engineering skill, designed by Robert Stephenson. The upper level, 112 ft. above high water mark, is used by the railway with a roadway hung below.[6] A line from Newcastle runs sixty-six miles west to Carlisle, while another runs east some twenty miles to Sunderland.

Newcastle is noted for its shipbuilding yards and manufacture of locomotives and its iron industry. But chiefly it is noted for its extensive mines and coal shipping. One recalls the old adage about "bringing coals to Newcastle." It lies nine miles from the mouth of the Tyne. It was the terminus of our long day's journey of some two hundred sixty-nine miles from London.

[As we left Newcastle the next day and floated down the Tyne to the North Sea] in the darkness, unseen, we passed several interesting sites. One was Walls End, so called from its being the end of the great Roman Wall [Hadrian's Wall] built across Britain from the North Sea to the Irish Sea. The first wall was an earthen rampart replaced later by a stone wall eight feet thick and twelve feet high, (probably) by Em-

5. Pons Aelius (or Newcastle Roman Fort) was another fort and small Roman settlement on Hadrian's Wall (www.roman-britain.org/places/pons_aelius.htm).

6. Designed by Robert Stephenson and built between 1847 and 1849, Newcastle's High Level Bridge is the first major example of a wrought-iron, tied-arch (or bowstring) girder bridge. It spans 1,337 feet of river valley, including 512 feet across water (John Addyman and Bill Fawcett, *The High Level Bridge and Newcastle Central Station — 150 Years across the Tyne* [North Eastern Railway Association, 1999]).

peror Severus about A.D. 208. This was guarded by 18 military stations, garrisoned by cohorts of Roman soldiers. At intervals of a mile were forts (80 in all containing 80 men each), and between each pair of forts were four watch towers.[7] At Jarrow are a few fragments of the monastery of the Venerable Bede; and South Shields (pop. over 100,000) and Tynemouth (pop. nearly 60,000) are important seaports.

7. Although Anderson never saw Hadrian's Wall in more than brief glimpses, its fascinating history was magnetic to him. It is a stone and turf boundary fortification built across the width of what is now northern England. Begun in 122 CE, during the rule of Roman Emperor Hadrian, it was the third of four such fortifications built across Great Britain to prevent military raids by the ancient inhabitants of Scotland to the north, promote peaceful conditions and economic stability, and mark the frontier of the Empire. A significant portion of the wall still exists, and for much of its length it can be followed on foot. The best-known historic attraction in northern England, it was designated a UNESCO World Heritage Site in 1987.

A Treatise on "The Cootie"

Godfrey Anderson

EVERY AMERICAN SOLDIER is now familiar with that species of insect vulgarly known as the cootie. It requires no introduction, introducing itself quite readily. Clinging with remarkable tenacity, this ferocious little beast is usually to be found lurking in the innermost recesses of one's B.V.D.'s, where he maintains a system of slow but nonetheless diabolical cannibalism. For he is a MANEATER, possessed of an insatiable and unquenchable thirst for human gore.

This inhuman monster, plainly visible to the naked eye, is of itself transparent. But upon having indulged in one of his usually gluttonous orgies, and filled his digestive apparatus with human blood, one can make out the location of his dinner as one can locate the yolk of an egg upon holding the latter against the light.

The usual symptoms of the presence of this unwelcome visitor [are] a general feeling of discomfort accompanied or followed by local itching. There is usually present an overwhelming desire to scratch the afflicted parts with the nails of the fingers, and in extreme cases the temptation to indulge in profanity is altogether irresistible.

The proper method of procedure is thus: strip to the waist and

---

Originally published in the *Sentinel*, a U.S. armed forces journal published in Archangel, Russia.

dexterously invert the undershirt. Then examine carefully the seams and the adjacent area, where they usually lurk about on ambush, ready to spring forth, foam-beflecked, with bloodshot eyes and with a frightful ear-splitting, gnashing of teeth — in short, in all their hideous malevolence.

Frequently, however, the cootie will resort to subtle strategy. Finding himself suddenly beset by an implacable foe, subject to sure and speedy annihilation upon discovery, he will feign death with amazing reality, even to the glassy stare of the eyeballs, seeking by means of this simple ruse to escape an awful fate. Were it not for the violent pounding of his heart and an uncontrollable spasmodic agitation of the Adam's apple, due no doubt to the awful mental strain of this precarious position, his acting would attain a perfection likely to cause Shakespeare himself to squirm and wiggle about in his tomb.

Having trailed the cootie to his lair, it now behooves us to exterminate him. There are several methods of procedure. A very successful one is to present a loaded rifle at his head and pull the trigger. If carried out successfully, death should ensue instantaneously, if not at once. Another splendid method of extermination is to steal cautiously upon the cootie, in ambush, and toss a lasso about his neck. Taken thus unawares, and while [he is] stupefied with surprise, it is very easy to bind the monster hand and foot, and place his head upon an anvil. Grasping a 7-pound coke hammer firmly in both hands, proceed to deliver a rapid succession of violent blows upon the cranium, and presently your patience will be rewarded by hearing a sickening crunch of bones, signifying that his skull is crushed and life is extinct.

Two Poems about the "Polar Bears"

This first poem, written by George Smith in early 1919, speaks to the concerns of the many families in Michigan who wanted their husbands, sons, and fathers to come home from Russia — and soon — because the armistice ending World War I had been declared. From their perspective, the risks facing the North Russia Expeditionary Force were too great for any benefit the United States and the Allies might gain. The poem was published in the *Detroit News* in February 1919; it was reprinted in *Michigan History Magazine* (83, no. 1 [1999]: 32).

What about Bringing Them Home?

Did we declare war upon Russia
When we took a hand in the game?
I know that we hopped onto Prussia,
And Austria got it the same.
But still I have no recollection
Of breaking with Russia, I swear,

And cannot help making objection,
To having our boys over there.

What quarrel have we with that nation?
Just how did it tread on our toes?
We prate of our friendly relation,
Then how can we class them as foes?
I'll back up most any complete fight,
So long as we really make war,
But this is too much like a street fight,
And nobody knows what it's for.

I know that a red reign of terror
Is flaming throughout Russia today,
But still I insist it an error
To bring Yankee troops into play.
We wound up the big war in Europe,
We settled the major campaign,
Then why should they ask us to cure up
The testers that seem to remain?

It's Europe's own fight we are waging,
For we're at war with the Russ.
And what is the sense of engaging
In something that doesn't affect us?
Our own boys have tackled a struggle
That no one should ask them to bear.
Their lives are too precious to juggle,
Now, why are they fighting out there?

We say that the struggle is finished,
We say that the war has been won,
The army will soon be diminished.
The boys who demolished the Hun
To all of their home folks are writing,
"We'll soon be recrossing the foam."

Then why are these other boys fighting?
And, what about bringing them home?

The second poem was written by Sergeant Roger Clark, one of the Polar Bears stationed in Archangel, on the occasion of their first and only Christmas (1918) in Russia. Like many other communications from soldiers during wartime, it has a more lighthearted and sarcastic tone than the first poem, a tone in character with Godfrey Anderson's in his "treatise on the cootie" (Appendix C above).

Quartered in Hell

When the Lord was designing Creation,
and laying out oceans and lands,
with never an hour's relaxation,
nor a moment to spit on His hands,
as anyone will in a hurry,
He let things get by now and then
in all the excitement and worry
that He should have done over again.

So, rather than mess up the outfit,
He saved every blunder and blob,
and laid them aside in the corner
to use at the end of the job.
The sixth afternoon of the contract,
the bonus expiring that day,
He bailed out the dregs of Creation
and shoveled the litter away.

He scraped all the wreckage and tailings
and sewage and scum of the sump,

and made on the shores of the Arctic
a great international dump.
He rushed the thing through in a hurry,
and because of the rush He was in,
He named the locality Russia,
and Russia it has always been.

And then, feeling glum and sarcastic,
because it was Saturday night,
He spotted the nastiest corner
and called it "Archangel," for spite!
It is there they do everything backwards,
and mud doesn't dry between rains,
where money and sawdust are plenty,
and thievery is better than brains.

It's the home of the glop and the bo-hunk,
and herring, and mud-colored crows.
My strongest impression of Russia
gets into my head through my nose!
It's the land of the infernal odor,
the land of the national smell,
the average American soldier
would rather be quartered in Hell!

It's back to the states for "Yours Truly"
a sadder but wiser young chap,
The Lord played a joke on Creation,
when Russia was dumped on the map!

Sergeant Roger S. Clark
310th US Army Engineers
Archangel, Russia
Christmas, 1918

Bibliography

Secondary Sources

Bozich, Stanley J., and Jon R. Bozich. *"Detroit's Own" Polar Bears: The American North Russian Expeditionary Forces, 1918-1919.* Detroit: Polar Bear Publishing Co., 1985.

Carey, Neil G. *Fighting the Bolsheviks.* Novata, CA: Presidio, 1997.

Chew, Allen F. "Fighting the Russians in Winter: Three Case Studies." Fort Leavenworth, KS. Combat Studies Institute, U.S. Army Command and General Staff College, 1981: https://cgsc.leavenworth.army.mil/carl/resources/csi/Chew/CHEW.asp.

A Chronicler [John Cudahy]. *Archangel: The American War with Russia.* Chicago: A. C. McClurg & Co., 1924.

Crownover, Richard. *The United States Intervention in North Russia — 1918, 1919: The Polar Bear Odyssey.* Ceredigion, UK: Edwin Mellen Press, 2001. [DVD copies of an April 16, 2008, lecture at the Troy Museum and Historic Village by Richard Crownover are available for $25 by calling Cindy Stewart at (248) 524-1147.]

Fogelsong, David S. *America's Secret War against Bolshevism.* Chapel Hill: University of North Carolina Press, 1995.

Goldhurst, Richard. *The Midnight War.* New York: McGraw-Hill, 1978.

Gordon, Dennis. *Quartered in Hell: The Story of American North Russian Expeditionary Force, 1918-1919.* Missoula, MT: Doughboy Historical Society and G.O.S., Inc., 1982.

Graves, Gen. William S. *America's Siberian Adventure.* New York: Jonathan Cape and Harrison Smith, Inc., 1931.

Halliday, E. M. *When Hell Froze Over.* New York: Ibooks, Inc., 2000 (originally published as *The Ignorant Armies.* New York: Simon and Schuster, 1958).

Hudson, Miles. *Intervention in Russia, 1918-1920: A Cautionary Tale.* South Yorkshire, UK: Pen and Sword, 2004.

Ironside, Gen. Edmund. *Archangel, 1918-19.* London: Constable & Co., 1953.

Kennan, George F. *The Decision to Intervene: Soviet-American Relations, 1917-1920.* Vol. 2. Princeton, NJ: Princeton University Press, 1958.

Kettle, Michael. *Churchill and the Archangel Fiasco: November 1918–July 1919.* Oxford: Routledge, 1992.

Moore, Joel R., Harry Mead, and Lewis E. Jahns. *The American Expedition Fighting the Bolsheviki: Campaigning in North Russia, 1918-1919.* Detroit: Polar Bear Press, 1920 (reprinted by the Battery Press, Nashville, 2003).

Moore, Perry. *Stamping out the Virus: Allied Intervention in the Russian Civil War, 1918-1920.* East Sussex, UK: Naval and Military Press, 2002.

Saul, Norman E. *War and Revolution: The United States and Russia, 1914-1921.* Lawrence: University Press of Kansas, 2001.

Somin, Ilya. *Stillborn Crusade: The Tragic Failure of Western Intervention in the Russian Civil War, 1918-1920.* New Brunswick, NJ: Transaction Publishers, 1996.

Wadley, Patricia L. "Even One Is Too Many." PhD diss., Texas Christian University, 1993. http://www.aiipowmia.com/research/wadley.html.

Willett, Robert L., Jr. *Russian Sideshow: America's Undeclared War, 1918-1920.* Washington, DC: Potomac Books, 2003.

York, Dorothea. *The Romance of Company "A," 339th Infantry, A.N.R.E.F.* Detroit: McIntyre Printing Co., ca. 1923.

Web sites

"339th Infantry Regiment in Northern Russia, 1918-1919." U.S. Army black-and-white silent film of the activities of the Polar Bears in North Russia shot by Signal Corps photographers. Available from: Traditions Military Videos, P.O. Box 656, Julian, CA 92036 (http://www.militaryvideo.com/store/store.cfm?titleID=339th&do=detail#long).

"American Sentinel," May 31, 1919. A digital copy of newspaper published by U.S. Army in Archangel, Russia, on May 31, 1919 (http://pbma.grobbel.org/photos/American_Sentinel_Page_01_resized.jpg (pp. 2-4, same url with altered page number).

"America's Secret War." Hundreds of AEF photos (http://secretwar.hhsweb.com/).

"Camp Custer, Battle Creek, Michigan." Collection of postcard images of Camp

Custer (http://freepages.military.rootsweb.ancestry.com/~worldwarone/
WWI/MilitaryCamps/CampCuster/index.html).

Canadian National Film Board. "Images of a Forgotten War." Archive of the Canadian Expeditionary Force WW I film footage is available for viewing on-
line: http://www3.nfb.ca/wwi/index.php.

"Chief Yeoman of Signals, George Smith, Royal Navy." Diary, photographs, mementos (http://www.naval-history.net/WW1z05NorthRussia.htm).

"'Detroit's Own' Polar Bear Memorial Association." Official Web site of the organization that is "dedicated to honoring and maintaining the memory of the
339th Infantry Regiment, the 1st Battalion of the 310th Engineers, the 337th
Ambulance Co. and the 337th Field Hospital of the U.S. Army's 85th Division" (http://pbma.grobbel.org).

"Ethelbert E. Daish's Diary: June 5th–October 17th 1919." Daish went to North
Russia on the hospital ship *London Belle* with the United Kingdom's North
Russia Expeditionary Force (http://myweb.tiscali.co.uk/bardenweb/).

"Historical Files of the American Expeditionary Force, North Russia, 1918-19."
Footnote.com, digitized National Archives Microfilm Publication M924: reports, studies, memoranda, and other records (http://www.footnote.com/
documents/19387125/us_expeditionary_force_north_russia).

Independence Seaport Museum, Philadelphia, home of the U.S.S. *Olympia*,
which delivered the first U.S. military forces to Archangel (http://www
.phillyseaport.org/historicships/olympia.html).

"The Journal and Photographs of Yeoman of Signals George Smith, Royal Navy"
(http://www.naval-history.net/WW1z05NorthRussia.htm).

"Meeting of Frontiers." Collections from the Library of Congress. William C.
Brumfield Collection (http://frontiers.loc.gov/intldl/mtfhtml/mfdigcol/
mfdcphot.html#a_eng).

"Modern Maps of the Area Where the 'Polar Bears' Fought." 2002 map of the region
near Archangel, Russia (copy in "Detroit's Own" Polar Bear Memorial Association: http://home.comcast.net/~mvgrobbel/military/ArchangelRegionMap.htm).

"North Russian Expeditionary Force 1919." Photos, information, and maps describing the British Royal Navy Operations in North Russia. Compiled by
George William Smith, Chief Yeoman of Signals, Royal Navy (http://
www.naval-history.net/WW1z05NorthRussia.htm).

"A 'Pathetic Sideshow' — Australians and the Russian Intervention, 1918-1919."
The Australian War Memorial Web site: http://www.awm.gov.au/encyclo-
pedia/north_russia/journal.asp.

"Photos from the Fronts." Twenty-first-century views courtesy of Mr. Alexey
Suhanovsky of Arkhangel'sk, Russia (http://pbma.grobbel.org/photos/
alexey/dvina.htm).

"Polar Bear Expedition Digital Collections." More than fifty individual collections of primary source material, including diaries, maps, correspondence, photographs, ephemera, printed materials, and a motion picture (http://polarbears.si.umich.edu/).

"A Polar Bear in North Russia." Photos and memorabilia from the scrapbook of William Bryan Robbins (http://ancestories1.blogspot.com/2007/07/polar-bear-in-north-russia.html).

The Story of the American Expeditionary Forces. Doughboy Center (http://www.worldwar1.com/dbc/p_bears.htm).

"World War I Document Archive." Primary documents from World War I (http://wwi.lib.byu.edu/index.php/Main_Page).

Articles

Crownover, Roger. "Stranded in Russia." *Michigan History Magazine* 83, no. 1 (Jan.-Feb. 1999): 28(16). General Reference Center Gold. Gale. Library of Michigan, 16 May 2009 (http://0-find.galegroup.com.elibrary.mel.org/itx/start.do?prodId=GRGM).

Grobbel, Mike. "The 'Polar Bears' of World War One — Remembering the Allied Intervention in North Russia." *Polar Bear News,* Dec. 2004–June 2005 (http://pbma.grobbel.org/westriding/polar_bear_news.htm).

Halliday, E. M. "Where Ignorant Armies Clashed by Night." *American Heritage Magazine,* Dec. 1958 (vol. 10, no.1) (http://www.americanheritage.com/articles/magazine/ah/1958/1/1958_1_26.shtml).

"Home from War." *Time,* Dec. 9, 1929 (no author). Return of remains of 75 U.S. soldiers (http://www.time.com/time/magazine/article/0,9171,738228-2,00.html).

Kramer, Andrew. "Centenarian Recalls Fighting Russians." AP article dated Aug. 8, 2001, Center for Defense Information (http://www.cdi.org/russia/johnson/5385.html##13).

Murchie, Guy, Jr. "Tragedy at Archangel — the Amazing Story of America's Futile Expedition into Bolshevik Land." *Chicago Sunday Tribune,* Graphic Section, Feb. 26, 1939 (http://home.comcast.net/~mvgrobbel/military/WWI/tragedyatarchangel.htm).

Zacharias, Pat. "Detroit's Polar Bears and Their Confusing War." *Detroit News,* July 22, 2000 (http://apps.detnews.com/apps/history/index.php?id=178).